WE CAME FIRST

For all the women, today and
tomorrow, who do things a
bit differently.

LAURENCE KING

Published in 2019
by Laurence King Publishing Ltd
361–373 City Road
London EC1V 1LR
Tel: +44 20 7841 6900
Fax: +44 20 7841 6910
E-mail: enquiries@laurenceking.com
www.laurenceking.com

A catalog record for this book is available
from the British Library.

ISBN: 978-1-78627-502-8

Design: Mariana Sameiro
Copy-editing: Jacquie Bloese
Proofreading: Angela Koo

Printed in Hong Kong

Laurence King Publishing is committed
to ethical and sustainable production.
We are proud participants in The Book
Chain Project ®
bookchainproject.com

WE CAME FIRST

Relationship Advice From Women Who Have Been There

Jennifer Wright

Illustrations by
Carly Jean Andrews

Laurence King Publishing

CONTENTS

INTRODUCTION

Some time ago a man named Craig on Twitter remarked, "I just wish we could go back to the early 1900s where women were actually women and didn't hate men."

Craig's going to be disappointed to discover that the lives of historical women prove him horribly wrong. Sad face.

There's absolutely nothing I hate more than the notion that the past was entirely filled with soft-spoken and unfailingly nurturing women. It's a lie nourished by Hollywood and perpetuated by advertising. And God knows it crops up any time a conservative newspaper columnist starts pining for "the good old days." I'm not alone in my loathing of this assumption; women like Emily Brontë didn't just hate men, she hated pretty much anyone who wasn't a pet or a family member (she told her young students that she preferred the school dog to them). I guess, to be fair, Mary Shelley, another woman of the 19th century, didn't hate men. She did, after all, store her dead husband's heart in her purse for safe-keeping, which is a mark of affection if ever I've heard one. Maybe this is the sort of devotion Craig was searching for?

The women of the past were anything but the doting caricatures they're often made out to be. They were under a lot of the same pressures when it came to dating and mating as modern women, and many of their solutions would be considered progressive, even by today's standards. Your lacklustre boyfriend? Your mixed feelings about children? Whether or not to host a massive orgy? They would have been able to advise you on all of that. Whether you'd have liked what they had to say is an entirely different matter.

But I love that their advice wouldn't necessarily have been great (I do not, personally, think you should dose a love rival with laxatives.) Some of them were forward looking. Some were traditionalists. Some believed that beauty was their greatest asset. Others would have found that notion infuriatingly stupid. Some of these women were amazingly pulled together, and some of them were really, really messy.

All of which is to say they were human. Each of them had their own likes and dislikes, turn-ons and turn-offs when it came to men. Or women. Until we engineer a time machine to ascertain all of these proclivities from the women themselves, this book will have to do.

I hope you can use it to dispel myths about dainty, delicate ladies of the olden days and champion the complicated love lives of the women who came first. In every sense of the phrase.

FLIRTING

—

The amuse bouche
of romance—a delightful
first taste of what
is to come

Cleopatra on

MAKING THE FIRST MOVE

DEAR CLEO,

So, there's this super sexy barista who works in a coffee shop near my apartment and he's as hot as my 8 AM cappuccino. I want to chat him up, but I tend to be a little bit on the shy side. Should I just hope he notices me? Should I approach him? Any advice for how to heat things up?

Coffee Talk

DEAR COFFEE TALK,

Of course you should approach him. I would say do it because it's the 21st century, but this strategy worked well for me 2000 years ago, too. When people didn't want me to meet Julius Caesar, I had myself smuggled to him in a bedroll. As that awesome wordsmith Plutarch pointed out— "It was by this device of Cleopatra's that Caesar was first captivated, for she showed herself to be a bold coquette."[1] Damn right.

When I met Mark Antony for the first time, I made quite the entrance. I went to him in a barge and surrounded myself with handsome young men, dressed as cupids. The word on the street was I looked like—"a goddess in gold."[2]

I understand that barges are hard to come by these days, but bedrolls may be more widely available. Find what works for you. Maybe that's wearing your fiercest outfit the next time you go into his coffee shop. Maybe it's buying him a triple-shot espresso. Maybe instead of your name, you give him your number. And remember that there's no shame in making the first move, and there never was.

Who makes it happen? You. You do.

I am Isis reborn; I am the living Nile.
Cleopatra

"There's no shame in making the first move, and there never was."

Profile

Baby, I'm a Queen. More specifically, I was the Queen of Egypt from 51–30 BCE and such was my allure and intellect that I rocked it! I've always been into men who can match me—I've had affairs with Julius Caesar and his second-in-command, Mark Antony. If you think you're on my level, I'm open to being the more beautiful half of our power couple.

Turn-ons
Friends, Romans, countrymen

Turn-offs
Asps

Sappho on

BEING SEEN

DEAR SAPPH,

I live in a really conservative town. Let me stress—really conservative. And I think I'm gay. There's a girl I have a crush on. A huge crush. I want to ask her out, but I'm worried about revealing my sexuality to my family. I don't see it going well and I'm worried that at the very least they will cry, or maybe try to convert me, or do something even worse. Do you have any advice on how to come out? Should I even come out?

Still,
Closeted

DEAR CLOSETED,

I am from Ancient Greece, from a time when people just straight up believed in witches. That was a thing. And I was out as *hell*. There wasn't much acceptance though. A Christian theologian described me as "a sex-crazed whore who sings of her own wantonness."[3] Well, what interesting woman wouldn't do the same? In the 11th century, Pope Gregory VII tried to burn all my works. For most of history, scholars have been trying to pretend that my numerous love poems to women were somehow about a chaste nonsexual love. None of this pressure stopped me from writing endless poems about how much I loved women.

People will try to tell you who you are, and how you should be, and who you should love. They have been trying to change women like you and me forever. Don't let them change you. Love who you love. Life is short. (I should know—I'm long dead.) How you come out doesn't matter. Announce it politely over dinner or dress up in a rainbow flag. But tell people. Otherwise you have no defenses when they try to write your life for you.

Tell people who you are so others will know they are not alone. Your future girlfriend would probably appreciate your honesty, too.

Remember—"What cannot be said will be wept."[4]

Love you,
Sappho

"Don't let them change you. Love who you love."

Profile

Women For Women. Just so you know, the term "Sapphic" started with me. I come from the Greek island of Lesbos. If you are my beloved, I'll write you a ton of lyric poems, just as I did in the 7th century BCE. If you don't want to be my beloved, I'll still write you a ton of poems.

Turn-ons

Tropical islands with alcoholic beverages

Turn-offs

Men

Agnès Sorel on
BODY POSITIVITY

DEAR AGNÈS,

Do you have any tips for first-date attire? I have a dress that shows off a good bit of cleavage. I love my breasts and the dress is fabulous, but I'm worried that it will make me seem slutty or too easy. Should I cover up or flaunt myself? How much is too much?

Chastity A. Blaze

DEAR CHASTITY,

I'd recommend showing your breasts. Full on. Seriously. I had my dresses tailored to expose my left breast. And this was during a century when women weren't even allowed to show off their *hair*.

It made the writer Jean Juvenal super mad, and he told anyone who would listen about how "the king should prohibit openings in front through which you can see the women's nipples and breasts ... because they are so displeasing to God and the world."[5]

There are always going to be haters who are angry at women for having bodies. But who cares? You can see my breasts all over the place in paintings from that period "served up like a piece of fruit," as someone once said.[6]

The chronicler Georges Chastellain complimented me by saying "Of all that can lead to debauchery and dissoluteness in the matter of costume, she was the begetter and inventor."[7]

On that note: Be proud of your body. If you want to cover it up, that's great, but if you want to flaunt it in all its womanly glory, that's great too.

This strategy worked incredibly well for me; I acquired handsome estates, and gave birth to three of the King's daughters. There's no reason it can't work for you, too. (Note that I was poisoned in the end, though. Watch out for the jealous types.)

Agnès, Dame de beauté

Profile

Modest and demure are not words often used to describe me. In fact, one medieval scholar called me "France's first bimbo."[8] I was also the first officially recognized mistress of France, being *very* close to King Charles VII. Bimbos are generally smarter than everyone thinks.

Turn-ons

Diamonds, country estates

Turn-offs

Body shaming, all kinds of shaming, mercury poisoning

"Be proud of your body."

Nell Gwynn on

DEALING WITH THE COMPETITION

DEAR NELL,

I'm in a real predicament. I have a crush on a man who seems great, but he already has a girlfriend. I really, really feel that he and I would be a better match, but trying to steal him away from his current partner feels tacky and immoral. But then, can you really steal someone? Are there circumstances under which it would it be okay to pursue him? I guess I'm just,

Conflicted

DEAR CONFLICTED,

Poison her food. Don't kill her. Just lace it with laxatives before they go out on their next date. That's what I did to Charles's mistress, Moll Davis.[9] I invited her to a lunch fortified with laxatives; she spent the night on the chamber pot rather than in the King's bed. And then I swooped in like the kind of sexy angel who also poisons people.

Was it wrong? I mean, is all fair in love and war? I don't know. But I think a thorough cleanse is fine. And besides, you can't steal a man. He's not a flower pot. You must only look for ways to make yourself seem more appealing.

And my plan worked out *great*. I remained the King's mistress for seventeen years and my boys were given royal titles. People are still writing books and making movies about me. No one remembers to include the laxative incident, though.

Nell

"You can't steal a man. He's not a flower pot."

Profile

Samuel Pepys called me "pretty, witty Nell" and this description has held up through the centuries. Mine is a classic rags-to-riches story. I went from selling oranges at the King's Theatre in London to becoming the long-time mistress of King Charles II. He liked my wares. If you don't, then don't shake my tree.

Turn-ons

The Reformation, liberal ideas, the theater, fruit

Turn-offs

Civil War

Harriette Wilson on

ROARING WITH LAUGHTER

DEAR HARRIETTE,

So, I read a book of dating advice that told me to avoid telling jokes with men. I was surprised because I love jokes. I love making them; I love hearing them. However, I've read articles and tweets by stupid, horrible men declaring that women aren't funny. (First off, these men always seem to have a humor bypass, and who asked them anyway?) In any event, should I tone down my sense of humor on a first date? Will it alienate men if I'm funnier than them?

Funny Girl

DEAR FUNNY,

Joking will help identify idiots who need alienating. Any man who is even a little bit secure in his masculinity will love a sense of humor and not be threatened by it. I made fun of the Duke of Wellington constantly. It did not stop him from falling in love with me.

This piece of bedchamber pillow talk particularly sticks in my mind.

Duke of Wellington: I wonder you do not get married, Harriette!

Me: Why so?

Him: I was thinking of you last night, after I got into bed.

Me: How very polite to the duchess. [Pause] Apropos of marriage, Duke, how do *you* like it?"[10]

Making jokes, *even at a man's expense,* never impeded me one bit. I did it too many times to count.

And remember, all dates—*especially* the bad ones—are fodder for your own hilarious memoirs one day. Go girl—make them laugh!

Harriette

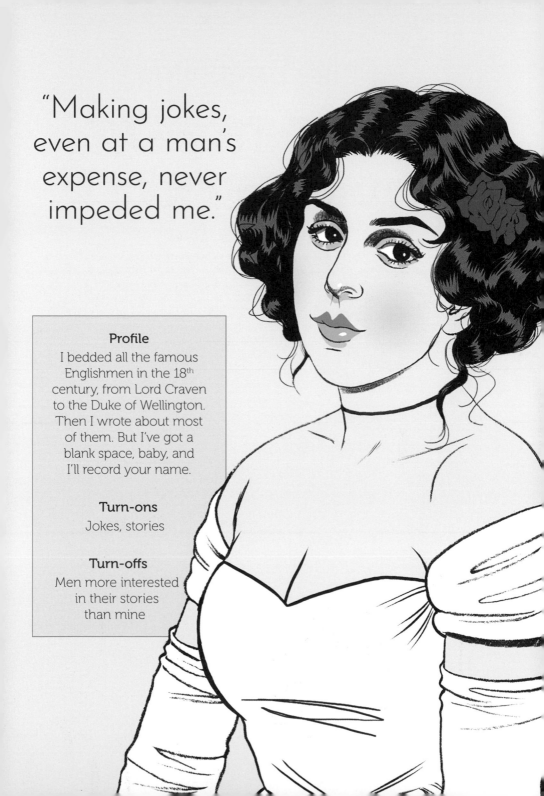

"Making jokes, even at a man's expense, never impeded me."

Profile
I bedded all the famous Englishmen in the 18th century, from Lord Craven to the Duke of Wellington. Then I wrote about most of them. But I've got a blank space, baby, and I'll record your name.

Turn-ons
Jokes, stories

Turn-offs
Men more interested in their stories than mine

Giulia Beneni on
GETTING WHAT YOU DESERVE

DEAR GIULIA,

There's this person I'm interested in. We have had a few amazing dates! Our chemistry is great. And I keep messaging and he gets back to me maybe fifty percent of the time. He says he is not looking for a serious relationship right now. He wants to keep hanging out, though, and he calls me in the middle of the night, so ... what does he want?

Hanging On, Hanging Out

DEAR HANGING,

Who cares what he wants! You deserve someone who is one hundred percent into you. He should be willing to do crazy things to win your affection. You should be able to ask for anything. I remember when I was living on the Champs-Élysées in Paris, a cavalry captain was desperate to sleep with me. He kept pestering to see me naked. I told him I'd bare all, if first he rode naked down the street like Lady Godiva. He did, with his troops behind him.[11]

That's what you have a right to expect in terms of devotion. Maybe with less nakedness. I don't know if that's your thing. I encourage "surprise" nudity. A suitor should be crazy stupid into you, at least at the very beginning. Ditch this lukewarm milquetoast and find a hot cavalry captain.

*Nakedly, honestly yours,
Giulia*

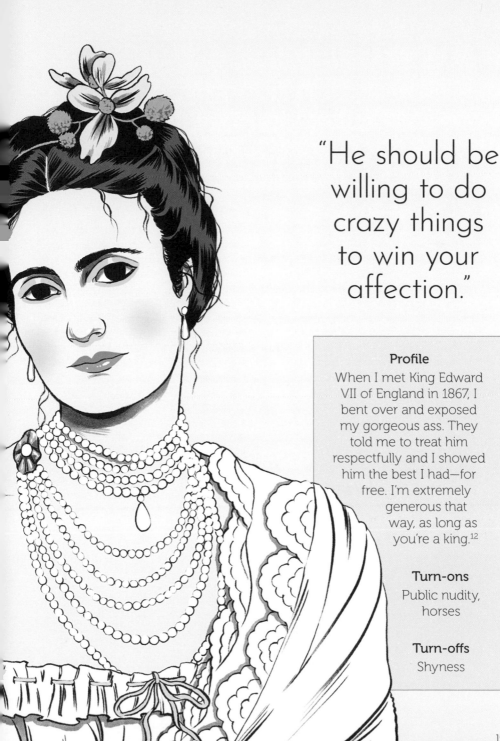

"He should be willing to do crazy things to win your affection."

Profile

When I met King Edward VII of England in 1867, I bent over and exposed my gorgeous ass. They told me to treat him respectfully and I showed him the best I had—for free. I'm extremely generous that way, as long as you're a king.[12]

Turn-ons

Public nudity, horses

Turn-offs

Shyness

Helen Keller on

DEFYING EXPECTATION

DEAR HELEN,

I'm writing to you because I feel hopeless. Not about everything. I have a wonderful support network in my life, but when it comes to love, I feel stuck. I have some health issues and physical difficulties that seem to make finding a partner harder for me. Meanwhile, all around me, people are coupling off, and it's hard not to feel resentful. And while everyone else is reassured that someone is out there waiting for them, no one ever tells me that. Am I just expected to...

Die Alone?

DEAR NEVER SAY DIE,

People didn't expect me to find love. People honestly didn't expect me to do anything. I was blind. I was deaf. Insofar as I interacted with men in my twenties it was because "a carefully set up photo of a radiant deaf, blind woman who looked neither blind nor deaf as she performed the turkey trot with a male partner could reassure the sentimental public that disability was not to be feared."[13] I was mostly okay with that.

And then, around 1913, I met a reporter for the *Boston Globe*, named Peter Fagan. We fell madly in love. But my family kept telling me "that marriage and child-bearing were not options for a deaf-blind woman."[14]

I wish they hadn't. I can tell you that, for me, love was truly a little island of joy.[15]

People will tell you that love is based on the eyes, that it's all about being immediately attracted to someone. Love—real love—goes beyond that. It lets you connect with someone else's heart.

I hope someone sees you as someone saw me. And as I saw him.

Helen

"Love was truly a little island of joy."

Profile
Deaf. Blind. Activist.
I suppose you're expecting
me to type something
like "aa;lskdjalksfjlafj."
Good one, never heard
that before.

Turn-ons
Touch—it's our
most under-
rated sense.

Turn-offs
People who are
horrible to
people like
me. I can't
see you, but
I see you.

Josephine Baker on
SLUT SHAMING

DEAR JOSEPHINE,

Does it really matter how many sexual partners you have? I'm worried I've had too many. To be honest, I may have lost count. Maybe I should lie about my dating history when I go out with men? I am pretty sure my current boyfriend is less experienced than I am. Should I at least tone down my exploits?

Too Much

DEAR TOO,

Does it matter how many times you've laughed? How many times you've danced? Or how many times you've watched the beauty of a sunset? Was your value as a human diminished by any of these things? I think not.

I'm writing as someone who danced topless in a banana skirt. Admittedly, I was never very inhibited. But I believe that sex is an activity that should be regarded as one of life's many joys, just like dancing![16] Who cares what other people think? One of my very own biographers said—"Baker would so actively engage in lovemaking that it resembled a gymnastics drill."[17] Do I give a damn? Nope.

Don't waste time with someone who judges you. You're more than just a number. You're a person, full of experiences.

Make them great.
Josephine

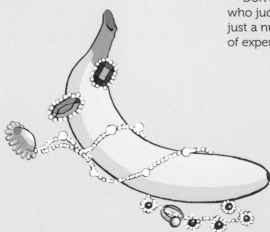

"Sex is an activity that should be regarded as one of life's many joys."

Profile

An American in Paris. I had two loves, my country and Paris[18]— and these loves made me both a scandalous dancer on the French stage and a passionate advocate for civil rights.

Turn-ons

Dancing in a skirt made of bananas, banana-shaped objects in general

Turn-offs

Racists. People who claim they're "not really racist" but do a great imitation of being racist

Kiki de Montparnasse on
SELF-EXPRESSION

DEAR KIKI,

I've been having a debate with a friend. I feel makeup gives me more confidence when I go out on dates. She swears that men really prefer a no-makeup look. Then again, every man I've met can't even tell when women are wearing makeup. I'm conflicted! If I want to appeal to men, should I opt to go fresh-faced more often? As a style icon, what are your thoughts?

Too Naked With A Bare Face

DEAR BARE,

I have no idea why you are even asking this. Your face is not for men. Your face is your canvas as an artist. Do you wish to leave it blank, exposing the stark simplicity of your soul? Do that.

I, however, was not a starkly simple person. Even as a child, I took geraniums from my mother's garden and crumbled them to apply a blush to my cheeks. I was fired from one job because I drew in my eyebrows with burned matchsticks. My lips were always bright scarlet.

All this embellishment brought me appreciation later in my life. The memoirist John Glasco called my makeup "a work of art in itself."[19] The artist Man Ray helped me craft my look, shaving off my eyebrows so they could be penciled in later to accommodate whatever look was desired. One day my eyelids might be colored copper for his photos; the next, an iridescent blue.[20]

I am universally beloved so I suppose you could just do what I did.

Sealed with a lipstick kiss,
Alice Ernestine Prin (Kiki)

"Your face is your canvas as an artist."

Profile
As a muse and artist, I've been called the Queen of Montparnasse. Looking for someone with a 1920s bohemian attitude, who is as inspirational as I am, with a butt to match.

Turn-ons
Closed doors—behind which anything can happen

Turn-offs
Closed minds—behind which nothing happens

Grace Kelly on

MAKING YOUR FEELINGS KNOWN

DEAR GRACE,

I have a friend who I'm interested in romantically. We get along great— we hang out, go to the movies, share selfies, etc. Lately, though, I've been wanting our relationship to go further. I think he might be interested as well, but I'm not sure. How I should bring this topic up? Or should I even talk about it? Maybe just kiss him? I don't know. But I bet you have a simply graceful (see what I did there?) way to handle this.

Am I,
Just A Friend?

DEAR FRIEND,

The next time he is at your place, suggest he make coffee. Go into the bathroom. Come out naked. It was my standard technique when I was interested in a man.[21] Trust me— he'll get the message. While a few of my lovers reported being surprised by this maneuver—because I guess it's not that "ladylike"—none of them seemed too upset. I have an inkling that your friend won't be either. And if he is, at least you will know the situation, and it's his loss, really. You can still have the coffee he made, so that's a result.

Gracefully yours,
Her Serene Highness, the
Princess of Monaco

"Trust me—
he'll get
the message."

Profile

Some would call me a bit of a princess, but I know at heart I'm just a humble movie star. In Alfred Hitchcock's movies I've been portrayed as an icy blonde, but if you're hot enough I bet you could warm me up.

Turn-ons

Frank Sinatra, Marlon Brando, Cary Grant, James Stewart, David Niven, Prince Aly Khan, Prince Rainier and (randomly) Bing Crosby

Turn-offs

People no one's heard of

WHICH FLIRTY ERA DO YOU BELONG TO?

1. Which body part would you flaunt to attract a new suitor?

A) A dainty ankle

B) My nipples. They're great. I don't do half measures.

C) My mind

D) My perfectly painted face is my trademark.

2. You're talking to someone fabulous at a party. You know it's going well when...

A) You discuss your dreams of the future.

B) You both joke back and forth.

C) You seem to have a deep intellectual connection.

D) They ask you to be their muse.

3. When is it a good time to get naked?

A) When I'm alone with a man.

B) Personally I like to expose just my breasts. Partial nudity is so much sexier.

C) When I'm alone with a man or a woman.

D) Onstage. I've got an amazing body and I want the world to see it.

4. How do you feel about soulmates?

A) I'm all about finding one true love.

B) Is that a kind of shoe?

C) I'm all about earth-shattering love, but it can happen more than once.

D) The very notion is bourgeois.

5. What's the sexiest trait in a partner?

A) Kindness

B) Power

C) Brilliance

D) Creativity

6. Who is your present-day celebrity crush?

A) Henry Cavill

B) George Clooney

C) Angelina Jolie

D) Oscar Isaac

7. What would you do if you found out the person you were pursuing already had a partner?

A) Be really sad, have a good cry, and then go on with life.

B) Put laxatives in his or her partner's food, and refuse to apologize for it.

C) Think on the situation and hope it inspires a poem.

D) Drink a lot, then have sex with a stranger to get over the loss.

8. What's your ideal date?

A) Going for a long walk and chatting a lot.

B) Food, fun, fucking

C) Hanging out someplace beachy where people bring cocktails.

D) Going to the theater or the opening of an art gallery.

9. What's your favorite emoji?

A) The heart

B) The eggplant

C) The ghost

D) The dancing girl

10. Do you ever want to get married?

A) I've been planning my fairy tale princess wedding since I was a child.

B) Like … why? Would there be a good reason?

C) Not really

D) Marriage is a trap.

Mostly As:
You belong in the incredibly repressed era that was early 20th-century America! One of the least flirtatious times or the least flirtatious time, at least when it came to acceptance of casual sex. But what it lacked in that regard, it made up for in longing looks and sweet conversations. Your flirting style is defined by a pleasing sensitivity, such as you might find in Helen Keller.

Mostly Bs:
You're all about having fun and hopefully being given a duchy in the process. You belong in the 17th century. You would be a sassy mistress for a king who appreciated your sharp wit and attitude. Also, like Nell Gwynn, you are very comfortable showing off your breasts, and that's cool—they look great!

Mostly Cs:
You belong in the ancient world, where, like Cleopatra and Sappho, you can relax in balmy locales, perhaps while composing poems about the object of your affection. You require a lover worthy of you intellectually, as well as physically. You would never refer to yourself as a sapiosexual, but you think that if anyone had that right, it would be you.

Mostly Ds:
You belong in 1920s Paris, drinking champagne. You would get along fabulously with other muses and performers like Kiki de Montparnasse and Josephine Baker. You're all about living life to the fullest and embracing creative outlets—while also having sex with whoever happens to be painting your picture at the time.

GOING STEADY

—

A tasty appetizer
that may not be
satisfying enough

Pope Joan on

SEX AND DEVOUT RELIGION

DEAR JOAN,

I'm in college and I'm still a virgin. My boyfriend and I have been together for a long time, but we are both from very religious, conservative families. My parents are convinced that college is a time where I should just devote myself to schoolwork and my future career. But I'm curious about sex, and I feel like it would be better to try it now, with someone I love. Any thoughts?

Virgin Unmarried

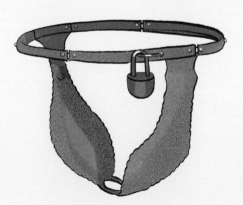

VIRGIN,

Do you want to destroy your career—and your life? Having sex surely ruined mine.

According to extremely contested, unofficial lore, I disguised myself as a man to train in the Church. I was so brilliant that by 855 CE, I was made Pope. But then I became pregnant. For a while, the robes really helped cover that situation up. I might have been able to hide my secret forever, had I not given birth during a papal parade.[1]

It would have been a less burdensome matter if I had gone on to have a super happy family, but, depending on who you listen to, I either died during childbirth or was stoned to death.

The sex may not have been that great either.

Also, if you have a child before you are married it *is* a bastard, and it *will* go to hell. You will probably also go to hell. Just FYI.

If you want different advice, seek out Josephine Baker or Nell Gwynn.

Blessings,
Pope Joan

P.S. Given that you're probably going to hell anyway, if you do have sex, use a condom.

"I disguised myself as a man to train in the Church."

Profile

It's said that every saint has a past, and every sinner has a future. As I was the pregnant Pope, circa 858 CE, I feel that holds up. Some say my life is so exciting that it can't be real. I say those people can't be serious. Hope you love kids and intense religious leanings.

Turns-ons

Loose flowing robes

Turn-offs

Parades. Not everyone loves a parade

Pocahontas on
HAVING A VOICE

DEAR POCAHONTAS,

First of all, love, love, love the Disney movie about you! So fun. I've been with my boyfriend about a year now. I love him, I really do. But he has just received a job offer that means leaving the country and he wants me to go with him. That's cool but I'm not sure how I feel about living in a place where I don't know the customs or speak the language. I'll be alone without any of my friends. I'd definitely have to quit my job and who knows how easy it would be to find another one? Then I remembered—you did it! How was it?

A broad abroad

GREETINGS BROAD,

YOU GET A CHOICE? I did not. I was separated from my children and family, kidnapped, and shipped to England, where I was forced to wear unfamiliar clothing that I routinely tore off[2]—I mean, have you seen 17th-century ruffs?

I was handled the way many exotic objects are treated—that is to say, as a "stick figure representing a race that was either barbaric or charming ... but never simply human."[3] I couldn't have put it better myself, TBH. And then I died at age twenty.

If anyone had asked, I would have preferred to stay with people who saw me as human and not as an object for their amusement. I would have preferred that a great deal.

No one asked.

I seriously can't believe you have a choice. Obviously, don't go overseas.

Also, my real name is—

Matoaka

"I would have preferred to stay with people who saw me as human and not as an object."

Profile
This is less a personal ad and more a cry for help. As the daughter of a Native American chief in the 17th century, I was raped, kidnapped, and dragged overseas. Weirdly, my life has become a Disney love story, where I paint with all the colors of the wind. Please help.

Turns-ons
Homeland, family

Turn-offs
Rape, kidnapping, English clothing

Lucrezia Borgia on
BEING A GOOD HOST

DEAR LUCREZIA,

My partner and I have been together for a long time. Our sex life is getting a bit stale. We want to mix things up a bit. Maybe more than a bit. We want to try having sex with other people. In a bigger way than a threesome. I've never had an orgy, but I know some friends who'd be up for the experience. Any tips on how to make this happen? I definitely want an event where everyone has a good time.

Swinging

DEAR SWINGING,

There's a famous, possibly apocryphal (I'm not telling) story shared by Renaissance chronicler Johann Burchard, whereby I sat beside my father (the Pope) and my brother at the infamous "Ballet of the Chestnuts." There, fifty of Rome's most beautiful prostitutes danced, then danced naked, then crawled around picking up chestnuts with their nether regions, and then had sex with men in attendance. We gave out prizes— "silken doublets, pairs of shoes, hats and other garments"[4]—to the men who had the most sex.

Whether or not this story is accurate, I'd say it's important to cultivate a fun and festive atmosphere at your orgy. The Ballet of the Chestnuts felt like it had the right vibe.

And consider prizes carefully—the more elaborate the better. Everyone likes a little motivation. Go nuts!

Also, remember women should receive prizes too. Especially if they're picking up anything on their hands and knees. Everyone should get rewards—like cool hats for exemplary sexual prowess.

Love, love, love,
Lucrezia

"It's important to cultivate a fun and festive atmosphere at your orgy."

Profile

I may be the daughter of a 15th-century pope, but I'm no angel. Unless it's a sexy Victoria's Secret kind of seraph. It's entirely possible that I'm that kind of angel.

Turns-ons

Love poems, power

Turn-offs

Poison—which I've found turns everyone off, forever.

Carolina Otero on
INDULGING YOUR APPETITE

DEAR LINA,

I'M GETTING MARRIED!
Super excited, as you can tell. I feel like I exist in all caps when I think about marrying the man I love, and getting to party with him and all our friends. But everywhere I look there's another article about how I can lose ten pounds before the big day—and I'm trying. However, I'm naturally curvy, and this wedding dress diet is killing me. Or should I say diets? I have tried Keto, and Atkins, and drinking Soylent, and that plan that Kate Middleton used. All that's happened so far is that I'm really cranky, which is a weird emotion to be feeling on the way to what's supposed to be a happy day. In your opinion ... is the pain worth the ten pounds?

Diet Disaster

DEAR DD,

Eat. Trust me, as a woman whose curves were fully appreciated, eating is one of life's great sensual pleasures. Colette once wrote that when I was eating, I emanated an air of "gentle bliss and ... happy innocence."[5]

And no, I was not eating kale.

I ate sausages and beef and chicken and strawberry ice cream at the meal with Colette, and I enjoyed four or five helpings. She marveled at my appetite. Honestly, it didn't even rival what some of my contemporaries ate—the Folies Bergère dancer Liane de Pougy used to serve peacock foie gras with champagne.[6] Some people will surely be amazed if they find out you are eating carbs before your wedding, but they will be hiding deep envy. They will call you "brave" without any discernable humor. But let me tell you, there is nothing more radiant than a woman enjoying herself.

I suppose the one "healthy" habit I had was that, after multiple helpings, I liked to dance. Given that you have a wedding coming up, perhaps you could eat what you like and practice your first dance steps with your fiancé afterward?

No more pain,
Lina

"Eating is one of life's great sensual pleasures."

Profile
Fondly referred to as "La Belle Otero," I'm a dancer, a courtesan, and a lover of life. I celebrate all that this banquet of life has to offer. Looking for someone to share my joy.

Turns-ons
Men who know how to cook, men who know how to serve, men who know how to do dishes

Turn-offs
The words "low fat" and "gluten free"

Consuelo Vanderbilt on

PUTTING YOURSELF FIRST

DEAR CONSUELO,

I've been dating my boyfriend for about three years. He wants to get married. But—I would <u>never</u> tell him this—I'm not sure he's THE ONE. And even if he is, we are still young. I want more time. The problem is my mother is super keen on the match. She keeps reminding me that he's wealthy and eligible, and that I'm not getting any younger! How much should you take your parent's input into account on matters of the heart?

Good Daughter

DEAR GOOD DAUGHTER,

DO NOT LISTEN TO YOUR MOTHER. I listened too much to mine and it led to romantic disaster. She insisted that I marry the ninth Duke of Marlborough, who I think was much more interested in my $20 million inheritance than he was in me. At the time, I was engaged to another man who I broke up with because my mother claimed my plans made her suffer a near fatal heart attack.[7]

The wedding was not what you'd call understated: four thousand people were invited and thousands crowded the streets to see me in my bridal attire. But I spent my wedding morning crying so hard no one dared approach me.[8]

I was miserable as a duchess. And bored. The marriage was annulled in 1926. My mother admitted that she'd forced me to marry the Duke, but she showed no signs of remorse. "I have always had absolute power over my daughter," she said. Thanks, Mom.[9]

Please DISCUSS it. Talk a lot. This is your life, not your mother's.

Love yourself first,
Consuelo

"This is your life, not your mother's."

Profile

I am a turn-of-the-century American princess, who became a British duchess. I found it to be a step down. I might be too rich for your blood, but how will you know unless you try?

Turns-ons

Making my own choices, rebelling against my mother

Turn-offs

Poorly heated castles

Wallis Simpson on

HAVING A SIGNATURE STYLE

DEAR DUCHESS,

I've been with the same person for years and our sex life has gotten tired. He's not as quick to rise as he used to be, if you know what I mean. Any suggestions on ways I can spice things up in the bedroom? People say you are renowned for having sexual dominion over men, so I'm asking for some fabulous royal sex tips, if you please.

A Real Snooze

DEAR SNOOZE,

Don't believe everything you hear. People have also said that I was a hermaphrodite witch...

Rumors about my amazing sexual prowess may—or may not—be true. But let me dispense some advice anyway. People often say that I caught the King's "attention" with a technique called either the Baltimore Grip (for my birthplace) or the Shanghai Clinch (for the years I spent in China supposedly, but improbably, frequenting brothels.)[10] You clench your vaginal muscles around a man's penis while he's inside of you. It's basically Kegels, but with another person. Supposedly, it greatly increases the man's satisfaction. I know in my partner's case, he had a lot of problems with staying aroused, and this seemed to be the only move that did the trick. It was ... gripping.

I'm not sure using my technique will make your boyfriend abdicate all his responsibilities for you, but you might as well give it a shot.

In retrospect, I should not have given the Nazis a shot, but that's not the question you posed.

Stay woke,
Wallis

"Rumors about my amazing sexual prowess may—or may not—be true."

Profile

King Edward VIII abdicated the English throne for me. If that seems like a sacrifice, then you've never tasted one of my martinis or enjoyed what I have to offer in the bedroom.

Turn-ons

Martinis, gin, getting kings to abdicate

Turn-offs

Being (correctly) told I'm a Nazi sympathizer

43

Amelia Earhart on

KEEPING YOUR IDENTITY

DEAR AMELIA EARHART/ MRS. GEORGE PUTNAM,

I'm engaged and really excited about the upcoming nuptials, but I'm not sure what to do about changing my name.
I love my name. I've worked for a long time to build up a professional reputation under this name. More to the point, I don't want to lose my Google search results. However, some people seem to feel very strongly that if I don't take my husband's last name as my married name, it will be hurtful to my beloved and/or just extremely inconvenient to the world. I'm becoming increasingly worried that not taking on a new name will result in society's condemnation further down the road. For now I feel,

Nameless

DEAR NAMELESS,

Oh, brother. I can't believe women are still experiencing pressure to take their husband's name when they don't want to. I had to deal with this stress in 1932 when *The New York Times* insisted on referring to me as Mrs. George Putnam, despite the fact that both my husband and I told them to stop. I had to explain that the name I was born with was, as I imagine it is for you, "more convenient."[11] And besides, I liked my name.

As with all women, I had an identity outside my husband's life and one I cherished. I did not become a new person upon meeting him, as a new name might imply. I stayed, resolutely, myself. This was, after all, the woman he fell in love with, and the woman who is remembered.

Sincerely,
Amelia Earhart
(not Putnam)

"I stayed,
resolutely,
myself."

Profile

My high school yearbook described me as "A.E.—the girl in brown (her favorite color) who walks alone."[12] Since then, I have become the first woman to fly solo across the Atlantic. I'm open to company, though, and always on the lookout for new members of the mile-high club.

Turns-ons

Flying high, open marriage

Turn-offs

Getting lost, seafood

Zelda Fitzgerald on
BEING UNDERMINED

DEAR ZELDA,

I'm a young, aspiring writer and this well-known published author wants to marry me. He says he finds me really inspiring. I worry though, that if I marry him, I may finish up living vicariously through his accomplishments, instead of experiencing my own. But he is amazing and exciting, and it might be fun to be someone's muse.

Musing On Musedom

DEAR MUSING,

Oh, it *seems* like it could be fun, doesn't it? My husband made me into one of the iconic muses of the Roaring Twenties and declared me the original "flapper." In fact, when he sent me the first chapters of *This Side of Paradise*, he said that the heroine resembled me—"in more ways than four"[13] —and people agree that all his greatest female characters bear a marked resemblance to me.

All of this makes sense, because my husband kept stealing passages of my diaries to "flesh out" his heroines. When I reviewed *The Beautiful and Damned* for *The New York Tribune*, I noted that "plagiarism begins at home"[14] —because he'd cribbed so much from me!

It was charming for a while. It became far less attractive when I tried to write my own book and was forbidden from using my life experiences for it, as he wanted to write about them.

"Everything we have done is mine,"[15] he told me, when I challenged him on it. As I said, charming for a while...

I would advise waiting until you can have an equal partnership with someone who will see you as more than just a source for *their* inspiration.

(Also, in my experience, writers are alcoholics who will drive you mad, so perhaps avoid them altogether.)

Be your own muse.
Zelda

"Plagiarism begins at home."

Profile

You will never be bored, because I am never boring. I am much, much more than just F. Scott Fitzgerald's wife. Currently looking for someone who can amuse me rather than make me a muse.

Turns-ons

Martinis, dancing, lighting cigarettes with $5 bills, the roaring '20s, roaring (literally) at fools

Turn-offs

Depression: national and personal

Anaïs Nin on

OPENING UP YOUR RELATIONSHIP

DEAR ANAÏS,

I'm in a long-term relationship, and I want to break out and try something new. Or rather, someone new. I'm intrigued by the idea of a threesome. I think it could be a liberating experience, but I'm also worried that adding another person into the mix might create a difficult situation between me and my partner. Do you have any thoughts on a ménage à trois?

Three's Company

DEAR THREE,

I have enough thoughts on this topic to fill a book, which, indeed, I have done. My affair with Henry and June Miller was very inspirational, as follows—

"They fell on this, the three bodies in accord, moving against each other to feel breast against breast and belly against belly. They ceased to be three bodies. They became all mouths and fingers and tongues and sense."[16]

In my opinion, threesomes are fun.

That said, I was bestowing my female gifts on a couple, which might be more satisfying than incorporating someone new into your current LTR. After becoming intensely entwined, you might find you do not want to sit and have a civilized breakfast with the newcomer.

Also, my husband Hugo might not have been as crazy about my love affair as I was.

Then again—try it.

Conflicted,
Anaïs

"In my opinion, threesomes are fun."

Profile
As the author of short stories, poetry, and extreme erotica, I have a low tolerance for the humdrum and the banal. Join me for only the most extravagant and extraordinary of adventures.

Turns-ons
Extremes

Turn-offs
All things prudent

Marilyn Monroe on

PLEASING YOURSELF

DEAR MARILYN,

I love the man I'm seeing. He's really kind and smart and funny. But he's not doing it for me in bed. At least not so far. I'd like to orgasm, but I really don't want him to feel bad about this lack of success. How bad do you think it is to fake orgasms? Did you ever pretend with any of your lovers?

Some Like It At Least Lukewarm

LUKEWARM,

As I once said, if the Academy gave an Oscar for faking orgasms, I would be an undisputed winner. I have done some of my best acting, convincing my partners I was in the throes of ecstasy.[17]

So yes, I certainly know a thing or two about this topic. And I understand why you might want to pretend, especially if you're the kind of person who really wants to make other people happy. But you have to value *your* happiness, too. And your orgasm can be a source of so much pleasure.

Personally, I didn't have an orgasm for years. My psychiatrist told me how to stimulate myself, so I would know the sensation, and only after that did I start enjoying myself with lovers. I never cried so hard as I did after my first orgasm. It was because of all the years I spent never having one. What a waste.[18]

Don't squander your time. There is never enough of it. And you deserve to fill the years you have with tears of joy.

Kisses,
Marilyn

"I never cried
so hard as
I did after
my first
orgasm."

Profile

Twentieth-century movie
star and sex goddess.
Like sex goddesses in
any century, I wasn't
guaranteed happiness, just
immortality. I've always
said that friends accept
you the way you are[19] and
I'm looking for someone
who can do that for me.

Turns-ons

Champagne, poetry,
marriage, the promise
of eternal love

Turn-offs

Cruelty to animals

WHAT WILL YOUR ENGAGEMENT RING LOOK LIKE?

1. How do you feel about diamonds?

A) I love bling. I'd have a diamond bikini if I could.

B) Um, you know they're worthless rocks that colonizers exploit native populations to procure, right?

C) I like all manner of stones, the bolder the better.

D) Don't they signify impending marriage? I do not want to get married.

2. What's your favorite sex position?

A) One where I can wear very elaborate lingerie.

B) Something with me on top, so I'm not held down.

C) Bathtub sex. Wet and wild.

D) The kind that definitely does not make me pregnant.

3. What item of jewelry do you always wear?

A) Big pearl earrings or a necklace

B) A piece with sentimental value, something from my parents or children

C) Always wear? I'd never be so predictable.

D) A big, bold cross

4. What's your favorite color?

A) Gold. Barring that, silver. Barring that, sparkle.

B) Colors of the wind

C) Rainbow

D) White

5. What color nail polish do you pick to complement your jewelry/ring?

A) Pale pink. Always be elegant.

B) I don't want those chemicals anywhere near me.

C) Bright green. Never be predictable.

D) Clear

6. What does your ideal wedding attire look like?

A) A long, flowing gown, trimmed with the most delicate lace

B) Something not too confining that I can run around in

C) A short, sexy dress that's good for dancing

D) I prefer clothing tailored for a man.

7. Where are you hosting your dream wedding?

A) My usual place of worship, with a reception at my family's home afterward.

B) An outdoor wedding, all the way

C) The Plaza Hotel

D) A church, of course

8. Which wedding beverages are you wrapping your bejeweled fingers around?

A) Champagne

B) A local specialty

C) A martini

D) Wine. (As in Communion wine.)

9. What would be your least favorite location for a honeymoon?

A) The cold English countryside

B) England. The whole country.

C) It's hard to say, but, I guess, England.

D) Hell, which is a real place.

10. What is your favorite Instagram filter for picking up your jewelry's glitter?

A) Willow

B) Nashville

C) X-Pro II

D) Instagram is the devil—I don't go near it.

Mostly As:
You're a modern-day Consuelo Vanderbilt, right down to the diamond-studded undergarments. Your diamond ring will be princess cut and enormous. Remember that all the diamonds in the world can't buy you happiness, but they can at least give you something sparkly to look at instead of your dull husband.

Mostly Bs:
Like Pocahontas, you're no fan of Western Imperialism and the conflict it can bring. Ideally, your ring would speak to your heritage—which may not involve diamonds at all.

Mostly Cs:
You're going to kick up your heels like Zelda Fitzgerald, and you need a ring as over-the-top glamorous as you are. Pick a vintage Art Deco setting, possibly with some colorful gemstones to set off your diamond ring, and party like it's 1920!

Mostly Ds:
Ah, like (the possibly fictitious) Pope Joan, you are really focused on your job right now. You're also absorbed in an old-school interpretation of religious texts. So, rather than an engagement ring, you will have a large cross.

MARRIAGE

—

The meaty,
sometimes monotonous,
sometimes fulfilling,
stew that makes up
the main course

Messalina on

ADULTERY

DEAR MESSALINA,

So, I'm thinking of having an affair. My tennis pro is incredibly hot; he seems into me, and my husband just isn't making much of an effort—in bed, or, to be honest, out of it. I'm young and I have needs. I'm pretty sure the tennis pro likes me. Any tips on how to handle this situation?

Lusty Young Wife

DEAR LYW,

Hey, fellow immoral woman! I have no problem with affairs. However, I cannot stress enough how discreet you should be. I didn't follow that advice, and it did not work out well.

I had plenty of affairs when I was married to Claudius but, with my lover Gaius Silius, who was remarkably handsome and popular, I wanted to go a step further. When Claudius was away on a trip to Ostia, I staged a spectacular public wedding to Gaius, with elaborate wedding attire, notable guests, and all associated fanfare. News about this event traveled fast. People honestly thought it might be a joke. Like, they thought I was getting married as a joke. The historian Tacitus noted that it was kind of amazing that anyone agreed to go to this wedding or officiate it at all.[1]

Claudius was not amused. He condemned me, Gaius, and all of our wedding guests to death. The wedding cake was good but I doubt anyone would have thought it was to die for.

We've all got to die sometime, but, in retrospect, I probably should have simply obtained a divorce. Have you considered that?

Messalina

"I cannot stress enough how discreet you should be."

Profile
I am the beautiful third wife of Emperor Claudius— but just because I'm married doesn't mean I can't have fun! That line of thinking will get me killed, so let's live for today.

Turn-ons
Public displays of affection, weddings, dancing

Turn-offs
Fidelity

Marguerite de Valois on
HANDLING IN-LAWS

DEAR MARGUERITE,

My mother-in-law hates me. She seems to take every opportunity to make it clear that I'm not good enough for her son. She hates my family. She hates the way I dress. She told him not to marry me. I've done everything I can to be nice to this woman, and nothing makes her like me. How can I win her over? Or, if I can't, how do I handle having this person in my life for the next 30 or 40 years?

Desperate Daughter-in-Law

DEAR DESPERATE,

Mother-in-laws, amirite?! When I was preparing to marry Henry, did my future mother-in-law, Jeanne d'Albret, ever talk shit about me. She complained about my makeup. And my dresses—or more specifically, my underwear. And how flirtatious I was. She said that I had "grown up in the most vicious and corrupt atmosphere imaginable" and couldn't see how anyone might "escape its poison."[2]

You know who didn't escape poison, according to many accounts? My future MIL. My mom took her shopping for gloves made by her personal perfumer, who had a reputation for being skilled with poisons. MIL died within a day. (I'm sure it was a total coincidence.)

I'm not saying that this is necessarily the best way to handle your difficulties. Just keep in mind your mother-in-law doesn't *have* to be in your life for 40 years. Talk to your own mom about what to do. She'll look out for you, just the way your MIL will for her son.

Bonne chance,
Marguerite

> "Your mother-in-law doesn't have to be in your life for 40 years."

Profile
Queen and licentious wife of Henry of Navarre (aka King Henry IV of France), I am the kind of girl your mother warned you about. Repeatedly.

Turn-ons
Sexy dress, sexy makeup, poetry, love letters, Paris, affairs

Turn-offs
Nagging family members, monotony

Marie Antoinette on

RISING TO THE OCCASION

DEAR MARIE ANTOINETTE,

I'm married to a really great guy. He's sweet, he's attentive, and we seem to have a lot in common. However, we didn't have any premarital sex, which I realize now was a big mistake. The problem is he's just not ... rising to the occasion. Is this normal? Is there anything I can do to coax him into action? I don't want to make a big deal out of it, but...

I Have Needs

CHÈRE I HAVE NEEDS,

I feel you on this. My own marriage to Louis XVI wasn't consummated for a full seven years. On our wedding night, he gorged himself even though his grandfather explicitly advised against it. My groom's reponse? "Why not? I always sleep better after a good supper."[3]

My mom really hated this situation—she wanted grandchildren to maintain the Franco-Austrian alliance—and suggested that I "lavish more caresses"[4] on him.

I'd just like to say loudly on behalf of daughters everywhere—IT TURNED OUT IT WASN'T MY FAULT, MOM.

Today, it's more often said that Louis suffered from phimosis, a condition that makes sex painful. It can be treated by circumcision, but back then there were no anaesthetics, so go figure...

So—back to my advice—if his heart is willing but his anatomy isn't, consult a doctor. It's more effective than my brother's stupid joke that Louis should have been "whipped so that he ejaculated out of sheer rage like a donkey."[5]

And if it's still not working out? You can always remain good friends and take a lover, as I did with Count Fersen.

Bisous,
votre Reine

"If his heart is willing but his anatomy isn't, consult a doctor."

Profile

A queen seeking a man who can keep his head in difficult situations. Fondness for gambling, fancy clothing, wigs, and pastries preferred.

Turn-ons

Role playing (I'm the shepherdess, usually.)

Turn-offs

Peasants. I find them revolting.

Queen Victoria on

MOTHERHOOD

DEAR VICTORIA,

My husband and I are planning to have a child! I'm 30 years old, we've been married for a year, and we're eager to start a family. But we're in the middle of a big move, and I'm worried about being pregnant while it's going on. Then again, I don't want to wait too long. When do you think is the best time to come off birth control?

Expecting To Be Expectant

DEAR EXPECTANT,

YOU HAVE BIRTH CONTROL? What is that? I did not have any of whatever kind of witchcraft you seem to be describing.

No one would tell me how to prevent unplanned births, so I had nine children. I DID NOT LIKE IT. I found all babies ugly, and having a large family was a huge inconvenience.[6] That was not the general attitude of my peers. Weird.

I also found breastfeeding disgusting, although my mother breastfed me, and my children also breastfed their offspring. Whatever. It's gross and women who do it are no better than animals.[7]

Anyhow, my children grew up, and they were fine, I guess (although admittedly, there is an enduring theory that my grandson was Jack the Ripper.[8])

I think the desire you're expressing for motherhood is insane. That probably means you will be better equipped for it than I ever was.

Please travel back through space and time and give me birth control.

Victoria Regina

"Please travel back through space and time and give me birth control."

Profile

I'm a one-man woman, so I think you're wasting your time with me. Wildly devoted to my beloved Albert, with whom I have sex constantly.

Turn-ons

Albert, sex, sex with Albert, being around Albert

Turn-offs

Men who are not Albert

Violet Gordon-Woodhouse on

FULFILLMENT

DEAR VIOLET,

So, a bit of an out-of-the-box question here—how do you feel about polygamy? I'm all for casual threesomes, but can a threesome sharing a house work? I've heard about the concept of having a "thrusband," and I'm pretty into it! I love the idea of having two men around, not just to sleep with, but to cook with and live with. Is it sustainable in practice?

Can't Stop At Just One

DEAR CAN'T STOP,

Ha ha ha. I had four husbands. I don't know if there's a catchy name for that? A "quadriage"? A ménage à cinq, I suppose.

This arrangement certainly worked out well for me. I would recommend finding a good mix so that no one is too similar—my husbands represented a range of professions and attitudes. One was a cavalry officer, one a lawyer, one a viscount's heir, and one a generous businessman.[9] They educated me, provided me with romance, and helped me progress musically. All understood that each of them was necessary to my happiness.

After all, no one person can fulfill every need, unless that person is me. I'm amazing that way. Sadly, I was only legally allowed to marry one of them, but they all claimed to be married to me. And we all lived together, quite happily, and quite openly, until death did us part.

Never stop.

Violet

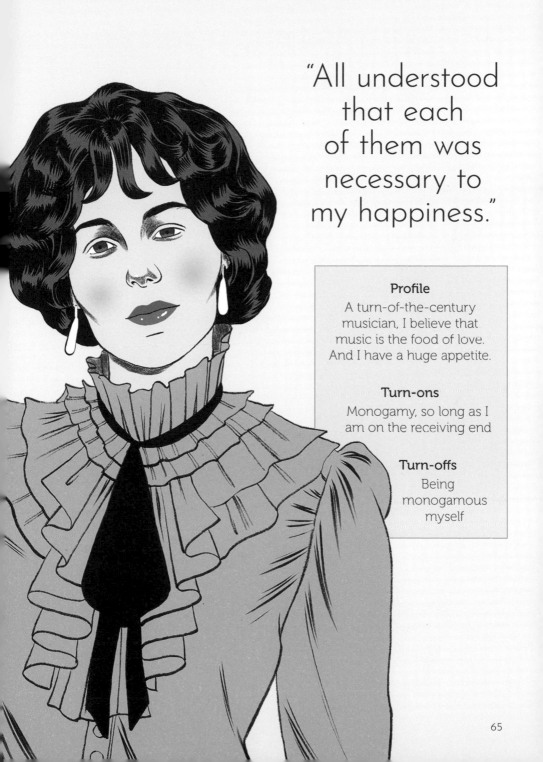

"All understood
that each
of them was
necessary to
my happiness."

Profile
A turn-of-the-century
musician, I believe that
music is the food of love.
And I have a huge appetite.

Turn-ons
Monogamy, so long as I
am on the receiving end

Turn-offs
Being
monogamous
myself

Eleanor Roosevelt on

KEEPING YOUR CAREER

DEAR ELEANOR,

I just married a man who holds rather traditional values. I have a demanding job, which I love, but it takes up a tremendous amount of my time. And we are now buying a house, which will take some work to renovate. I am wondering if I should leave my job and stay at home. My husband's in favor, but I'm not sure.

Book of Job

DEAR JOB,

Give up work? Are you mad? During World War I, I worked for the Red Cross and it was the most wonderful experience. I never looked back.

Being married is great, but it isn't necessarily enough to provide you with a sense of self. Even when my husband, FDR, became president, I never gave up working, penning a newspaper column entitled "My Day" from 1935 to 1962. I also hosted press conferences at the White House, which were only open to female reporters, thus forcing many newspapers to employ at least one woman.

I was once asked whether married women should hold jobs. I'll say the same now as I said back then— for some people, work is almost a necessity to development.[10]

Work if you love it. You can adjust your career to accommodate your schedule, but keep working. Do it for you.

Eleanor (aka Secret Service code name, Rover)

"Work is almost a necessity to development."

Profile

Big smile. Bigger heart. If you support UNICEF and believe in fighting tirelessly for civil rights, I am ready to rock your world! I wasn't just First Lady of America—Harry Truman dubbed me the First Lady of the World, and *Time* considered me one of the 25 most powerful women of the 20th century.

Turn-ons

Being a good person; everything else I can compromise on.

Turn-offs

Injustice, racism, Nazis—all the bad stuff

Lucy Hicks Anderson on

FIGHTING FOR YOUR RIGHTS

DEAR LUCY,

I'm transgender, and I live in a country where marriage to my partner isn't legal. For many people, my very existence is seen as an abomination, and there are still plenty of policies that discriminate against the transgender community. Many people who encounter me don't know that I'm transgender. I want to speak out about who I am, but I'm afraid it will make life for me and my family more difficult.

Transgressive

DEAR TRANS,

In my day, being known as a trans woman made life *very much* more difficult. I'm still proud to be who I am.

I was born biologically male, but that did not align with who I was on the inside. I had wished to be known as a girl since my school days, and I was fortunate to have a physician who suggested my mother raise me as female. I went on to live, dress, and act as what I am, a woman.[11]

And I lived like a fabulous woman. I ran a brothel and speakeasy all through the 1920s, patronized by the town's fanciest folk, and I was a well-liked hostess in my community. It was only after I married in 1944 that my problems began—I was tried for perjury because I'd "claimed" to be a woman when I got married. I went to court and stood up for our right as a couple to be married. I told reporters, "I defy any doctor in the world to prove that I am not a woman."[12] But I didn't succeed and was convicted of perjury.

The important thing is that I fought against discrimination. Ultimately, we moved to Los Angeles, where we lived peacefully until my death in 1954.

Never give up fighting for love and your right to happiness. Say who you are with pride, and in memory of those who came before you.

Lucy

"Say who you are with pride."

Profile
A 1950s transgender activist and all-round fabulous lady, I'm all the woman you can handle, and braver than any man you know.

Turn-ons
Liberty and justice for all

Turn-offs
People who do not believe in liberty and justice for all

Frida Kahlo on

HAVING YOUR OWN SPACE

DEAR FRIDA,

I love my husband—but I don't love living with my husband. He's a slob. I'm very neat. He leaves everything out, and I spend my time cleaning up, because the mess will drive me insane otherwise. We fight constantly these days. This was never a problem when we both had our own separate spaces. I dread turning into someone who nags him all the time. Do you think it's possible to be close with someone and also have your own space?

Home Alone

DEAR HOME,

Absolutely. I dearly loved my husband, Diego Rivera, but we had a very contentious relationship. We even divorced before remarrying the following year. I'm inclined to think our antagonism was all because of Diego's numerous affairs and not, as your problem seems to be, sloppiness, but I suppose multiple factors could have been at play.

We worked best when we could be close, but not on top of each other. Our architect correctly deduced that I should live alone.[13] But not *too* alone. That meant the construction of our twin houses in Mexico City, right next to each other. I had a blue one and Diego had a white one. They were joined by a rooftop bridge that led from my studio to his. We could visit one another when we wanted to, and flee one another when we wanted to.

Sometimes space is the best thing for a relationship, and for your soul. Find ways to be alone but not lonely.

Frida

"Find ways to be alone but not lonely."

Profile
"You deserve a lover who takes away the lies and brings you hope, coffee and poetry."[14] As an artist, I deal more with reality than hope, but I can definitely bring coffee.

Turn-ons
Flowers, jungles, freedom

Turn-offs
Cages, repression, Parisian intellectuals

Julia Child on

PRESERVING YOUR RELATIONSHIP

DEAR JULIA,

How do you feel about posting pictures of yourself and your partner on social media? My husband is worried we have an excess of lovey snaps online. I know some people complain about couples who take a lot of pictures, but I also like having a record of our love.

#Bae #Blessed #TrueLove

DEAR #,

Why shouldn't you have a record of your love?

Love is a most necessary ingredient in every aspect of life. When Paul and I were married we didn't have access to social media (and I'm still not sure I'm fond of blogs about my cookbook).[15] However, we did have cards. And what cards we sent. We were never organized enough to manage Christmas cards, so we opted to send Valentine's Day cards instead.[16] And the images were, if I say so myself, absolutely brilliant. There is one of us posing in a bubble bath. Another shows us as angels against stained glass. Another wearing cut-out hearts on our shirts. Today, some images are preserved on the Internet. It might be a tradition you and your partner want to adopt in the service of choosing quality of loving pictures over quantity.

Julia

P.S. Why does your name involve so many pound signs?

"Why shouldn't you have a record of your love?"

Profile
What's cooking, Good-looking? Searching for a partner who is willing to approach everything with zest. Food! Travel! Life! And love. Especially love. The pleasures of the table, and of life, are infinite. Bon appetit![17]

Turn-ons
Home-cooked meals, butter, France

Turn-offs
Microwaved dinners

WHO'S YOUR CELEBRITY PARTNER?

1. First things first: Do you have a type?

A) Brooding artists

B) Shy intellectuals (they're best at sex)

C) High-powered professionals

D) Bon vivant diplomats

2. Should they do the dishes?

A) I see us throwing dishes at each other as often as we wash them.

B) I'm sure we can hire someone to do dishes.

C) No, no, that's my job. Really, let me do it.

D) If I'm cooking, yes, of course.

3. How many times a week would you ideally have sex?

A) Are we fighting that week or making up? Probably on average 5.

B) One hundred. Just so much sex.

C) 3 or 4. Or zero when he's traveling. It depends.

D) 7. As dessert.

4. What would you do to cheer them up after a bad day?

A) Show them a photo you've posted where they look awesome

B) Suggest a night in with a good book

C) Massage their shoulders and remind them that they totally rule

D) Cook something delicious and comforting for dinner

5. What should your partner do to cheer you up after a bad day?

A) Gift me a new canvas or journal so that I can express how pissed I am in words/paint

B) Take me to a fabulous party

C) Show up with diamonds

D) Take me out to a French restaurant

6. Who's their historical crush?

A) A HISTORICAL CRUSH? BASTARD. WHO CARES. I'M GOING TO SLEEP WITH TROTSKY.

B) Ada Lovelace, the famed mathematician

C) Several

D) They only has eyes for me.

7. What are they wearing?

A) A hoodie

B) A tweed jacket

C) A dinner jacket

D) A button-down shirt

8. What are your partner's political affiliations?

A) Communist/radical/anarchist

B) Their privileged background shapes their world view. I'd say a left-leaning centrist.

C) They'd say libertarian, but I would say fascist. For some reason, this is desirable to me.

D) Left-leaning diplomat with a big heart

9. What's their favorite book?

A) *Catcher in the Rye*

B) *Infinite Jest*

C) *The Prince*

D) *The Amazing Adventures of Kavalier and Clay*

10. And their drink of choice?

A) Tequila

B) Coffee

C) Scotch

D) A glass of wine from a bottle you're sharing

Mostly As: Banksy

Congratulations! You should be married to a radical, somewhat reclusive artist who defies the bourgeois establishment, just like Frida Kahlo was to Diego Rivera. However, be careful that you direct your understandable anger at societal norms outward and not at one another.

Mostly Bs: Benedict Cumberbatch

There's something great about being with the smartest man in the room. Since it's hard to find world-famous mathematicians these days, you'll have to settle for a man who almost exclusively plays eccentric geniuses. He may not be Queen Victoria's husband, Prince Albert, but he is almost certainly going to play him in a movie someday.

Mostly Cs: Elon Musk

Genghis Khan conquered the world, and Elon Musk seems at least beginning to conquer space. Do keep in mind that relationships with someone who is laser-focused on their work can require an extremely understanding partner.

Mostly Ds: Tom Hanks

A truly nice, good man is the best. Paul, Julia Child's husband, was one. Tom Hanks seems to be another. You two can spend your weekends volunteering at soup kitchens and then taking nice walks through the park, or whatever else truly good people do.

BREAKUPS

—

A bitter sorbet,
to cleanse the palate
of what came before

Empress Josephine on

CELEBRATING DIVORCE

DEAR EMPRESS JOSEPHINE,

I'm getting divorced. It's not horrible. Well, it is kind of horrible (dismantling the house is horrible, figuring out who gets the dog is horrible . . . there are plenty of logistical horrors) but it really feels like it needed to happen. Possibly because we both kept cheating on each other—I'm sure you can relate. It feels weird to have no ceremony going out of this marriage, though. We entered it with a huge wedding, and now it feels like we're just slinking away in a courthouse. How do you feel about the idea of a "divorce party"? Are they super tacky or are they cool?

Party of One

Happy Divorce

DEAR PARTY OF ONE,

My divorce ceremony from Napoleon was beautiful. Like you, our parting came after a lot of living—on both sides. I became jealous and unhappy. We cheated on each other. And most importantly, I couldn't have children, and he needed an heir.

I was devastated when my husband suggested divorce, but the ceremony helped provide some much needed closure. We both read statements of devotion to each other. I mean, get this from my beloved ex-husband—

"Far from ever finding cause for complaint, I can to the contrary only congratulate myself on the devotion and tenderness of my beloved wife. She has adorned thirteen years of my life; the memory will always remain engraved on my heart."[1]

We kissed at the end of it all and, to Napoleon's credit, he made sure I was left with the financial means to live comfortably. We remained friends all the days of our lives.

And if no one can even remember Napoleon's next wife's name, that's beside the point. My advice is that if you think having a divorce ceremony will provide closure, I recommend it. It certainly helped me.

Affectueusement,
Josephine

Profile
Older and wiser. Totally
open to dating someone
shorter than me.
Especially if what he
lacks in stature, he makes
up for in ambition.

Turn-ons
Orgies, dancing semi-
naked, long love letters

Turn-offs
Disloyalty

"My divorce
ceremony from
Napoleon was
beautiful."

Lady Caroline Lamb on
ACCEPTANCE

DEAR CAROLINE,

I feel like I'm going crazy. A man I've been seeing for almost a year just broke up with me out of nowhere. I LOVE him. I don't care if people are telling me that there are more fish in the sea. He's the only fish I want. His birthday is coming up in a few weeks, and I'm still invited (as a friend) to attend. Is there any present (preferably for a moderate price) that you can think of that will show him that I still love him and that we are meant to be together?

I Gave Him My Heart

DEAR HEART,

You may have given him your heart, but may I suggest also giving him your pubic hair? After Byron and I broke up, I chopped some of mine off and sent it to him. I enclosed a letter asking him to send his own hair back, also warning him that I "cut the hair too close and bled."[2]

Lord Byron did not return hair of any kind, but he did send a locket, so that was ... well, many people would consider it a better gift.

Ultimately, we did not end up together, so take my advice with a grain of salt.

Caro

"We did not end up together, so take my advice with a grain of salt."

Profile

As mistress to Lord Byron, I proceeded to write poems and books about being mistress to Lord Byron. What's the opposite of an ice queen? I'm a passionate, "heart like a volcano" type, and I promise it's much more exciting.

Turn-ons

Men who are "mad, bad, and dangerous to know."[3]

Turn-offs

Boredom and predictability

George Sand on
TELLING YOUR TRUTH

DEAR GEORGE,

My partner has broken up with me. Was he a shitbag? Not in any especially abusive way, but right now I feel sure he was. He was definitely very annoying. And you know what, I want to tell everyone how horrible he is. Many people probably feel that's a tacky thing to do, though. I would like confirmation that using social media is completely fine before I post all of his failings on Twitter. Seriously, fuck that guy.

Secrets Are No Fun

DEAR SECRETS,

Lots of people think lots of things. You have a perfect right to tell your side of the story. If you don't, it's likely he will. Go ahead and share your feelings.

Take my ex, Chopin. Was he a bad guy? Probably not. Many reports will tell you that we mostly fought over how hard I was on my children, so I guess you could say he was a reasonably nice man. That's not how I told the story, though. In my novel *Lucrezia Floriani*, I describe myself as an angel whose only flaw is "loving too much." The book was about "what happens to all the rapture and the love when he who is the object of it behaves like a raving madman."[4]

Was that an accurate depiction of Chopin? Probably not! But he is dead and my book remains, so what's he going to say about it? Nothing, that's what.

George, a beautiful angel

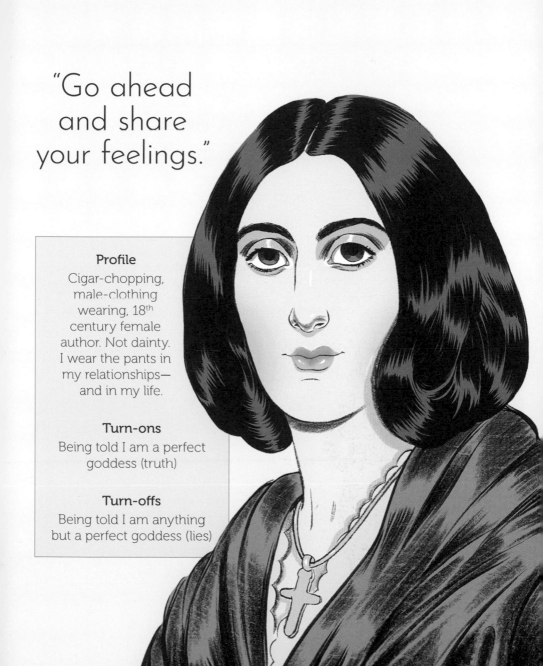

"Go ahead and share your feelings."

Profile
Cigar-chopping, male-clothing wearing, 18th century female author. Not dainty. I wear the pants in my relationships— and in my life.

Turn-ons
Being told I am a perfect goddess (truth)

Turn-offs
Being told I am anything but a perfect goddess (lies)

Victoria Woodhull on
EXPOSING ABUSE

DEAR VICTORIA,

I just went through a breakup with a man who was frighteningly abusive. I don't want to talk about what happened, but he is well known professionally and socially. I'm afraid he's going to repeat his actions with other women. Do I have a duty to tell people the truth about him? I'm worried that doing so will result in a lot of angry responses and accusations about my character.

Me, Too

DEAR ME, TOO,

I made it a personal mission in my life to expose men who did horrible things to women through my newspaper. In 1872, I got in particular trouble after my paper ran exposés on sexual scandals of the day. There was one article about a despicable man who raped two schoolgirls and afterwards "to prove that he seduced a virgin, carried for days on his finger, exhibiting in triumph, the red trophy of her virginity."[5]

I also told the truth about the adulterous affair of a popular (and extremely hypocritical) preacher. I was arrested on obscenity charges, because my words were deemed more offensive than men's actions.

I was comfortable being known as Mrs. Satan,[6] but it never felt exactly warranted. I wouldn't wish such a description on anyone. Speaking out does have consequences, sometimes frightening ones. And your actions may not get you much in the way of acclaim. But they will still deserve it. Be brave and do what is right.

Victoria

FUTURE
IS
FEMALE

"My words were deemed more offensive than men's actions."

Profile

Newspaper editor and the first woman to run for President—in 1870, fifty years before women could vote. They called me Mrs. Satan at the time. Looking for someone who is a hell of a good time.

Turn-ons

Any of those messages about how "the future is female"

Turn-offs

Anyone who still thinks "Mrs. Satan" is a reasonable way to describe female politicians

Dorothy Parker on
OVERCOMING HEARTBREAK

DEAR DOROTHY,

After three years together, my partner decided to ghost me! He just stopped replying to my texts, emails, and calls. It's like he dropped off the face of the earth. I don't know that I'll ever get over this loss. And for the time being, I can't stop talking about it. To everyone—my friends, my family, my therapist. I'm worried I'm becoming a broken record on the topic. How should I handle the fact that this breakup seems to consume my thoughts?

Parting Is Not Sweet Sorrow

SORROW—OR, SHOULD I SAY, SWEET,

Henry Miller wrote that "the best way to get over a woman is to turn her into literature." I was doing that with men long before he wrote those words.

You can't do much to rid yourself of heartbreak. However, you can turn it into something useful that will allow you to connect with other heartbroken souls. People are still reading my poems on the topic nearly a hundred years after I wrote them. Here's one for you that time does not wither, and which may help put your situation in perspective:

> *Sadly your banner fluttered down.*
> *Sullen the days, and dreary, dreary.*
> *(Which of the boys is still in town?)*
> *Radiant and sure, you came a-flying;*
> *Puzzled, you left on lagging feet.*
> *Slow in my breast, my heart is dying.*
> *(Nevertheless, a girl must eat.)* [7]

Now go out and inspire someone else.

Love and kisses,
Dottie

"Put your situation in perspective."

Greta Garbo on

BREAKING AN ENGAGEMENT

DEAR GRETA,

I'm getting married and it's a disaster. I've realized this is all wrong for me. Maybe I want to be alone. Or maybe I just want this particular person to leave me alone. But the wedding date is set and all our friends are coming. Also, the wedding is tomorrow. I have to go through with it now, right?

Runaway Bride

DEAR RUNAWAY,

Run. Run away from this horrible situation. You think other women haven't run? I was briefly engaged to my acting partner, John Gilbert, who was, understandably, very excited. He arranged for us to have a double wedding no less, with the director King Vidor and the actress Eleanor Boardman, which of itself struck me as a nightmare.

In any event, the morning of the nuptials, I just didn't show up. Gilbert didn't respond well; in a fit of fury, he punched the boss of Metro-Goldwyn-Mayer in the face—a bad career move on his part.

That's the only thing I regret about the day, though. There is nothing like the solitude you feel in the presence of someone else. Better you enjoy the pleasure of your own company.

Greta

"Better you enjoy the pleasure of your own company."

Profile
Movie star of the '20s and '30s, known for my performances in the films *Queen Christina*, *Anna Karenina*, and *Grand Hotel*. Looking for a partner who's not too chatty. Actually—you know what? Never mind. I want to be alone.

Turn-ons
Solitude

Turn-offs
Other people

Martha Gellhorn on

NAILING YOUR CAREER

DEAR MARTHA,

My ex is destroying my life—or at least my career. We work in the same industry. He knows I've been looking at this new job, and he applied for the very same one. He's not more qualified, but he talks a great game, and frankly, he's male, so he got it instead of me. I'm sure he's only doing this to spite me. Am I allowed to kill him? How do I even respond? Seriously, can I kill him?

Love to Work

DEAR LOVE TO WORK,

First, it sounds like you dated a dirtbag who is intimidated by your career. I was married to Hemingway, so ditto. But might I recommend this as a time to swing for the fences professionally?

I was working for *Collier's* magazine during World War II and was expected to cover the D-Day invasion—that is, until my estranged husband, Ernest Hemingway, volunteered for the assignment. *He didn't even work for the magazine!* But he was the famous author Hemingway, so of course he was given the job.

HOWEVER, I was not easily deterred. I stowed away in the bathroom of a nursing ship so I could report from the beach. I was the only woman to offer a first-hand account of the invasion, and, by the way, my account is magnificent. It describes not just the men on the beach, but the nurses on the ship nervously painting their nails to kill time as they approached the shore.[9] Hemingway? He never even made it ashore.[10] Sometimes the best revenge is being better at your job.

Don't let the bastards get you down.

Martha

"Don't let the bastards get you down."

Profile
Author, travel writer, and one of the greatest war reporters of the 20th century. A sex bomb who's ready to make love instead of war.

Turn-ons
International drama

Turn-offs
Domestic drama

Oona O'Neill on
GHOSTING

DEAR OONA,

I've been dating a man for a few months but it's not working out. He's had to move away for work and, though we were going to try to do long distance, I'm just not feeling it. I don't want to make a long drive—or fly—or even phone to tell him we're breaking up. Can I—and I know this might be a controversial question—can I ghost him? I really don't want to have an awkward conversation with him.

Spirited

DEAR SPIRITED,

Only if you want him to be mad at you. Because he will be. Ghosting is the one way to make certain you're ultimately going to have an awkward conversation with him.

Believe me, I know. I tried this when I was dating Salinger. It wasn't that serious—I was also dating Orson Welles! I was a teenager, and Salinger was sent off to boot camp training for World War II. Being in a long-distance relationship doesn't really work, even if you're with someone who writes great love letters. I then started dating Chaplin and married him shortly afterward.

J.D. found out I was married in a newspaper article and behaved with about the level of upset you might expect. He wrote me a letter describing what my wedding night would be like with a man who was supposedly undergoing treatment for impotence using monkey glands.[11] He made a pornographic cartoon of Charlie and me and sent it to us. It made me glad I was with Charlie and not him.

For the record, Charlie and I had eight children, so if he was being treated with monkey glands, the treatment must have worked really well.

Take the time to call your soon-to-be ex and let him know it's over from you, not from another source.

Stay real.

Lady Chaplin

"Take the time to call your soon-to-be ex."

Profile
Daughter to playwright Eugene O'Neill. Girlfriend to author J.D. Salinger. Wife to actor and filmmaker Charlie Chaplin. Legendary in my own right. Expecting you to be as well.

Turn-ons
Genius. Experience. Humor.

Turn-offs
Phonies who are always writing about how fake everyone is. They're not as smart as they think they are.

Jackie Kennedy on

DEALING WITH INFIDELITY

DEAR JACKIE,

My husband is cheating on me. I know this for a fact. I knew of his "wandering eye" before we married, but now it's eating me up inside. I'm trying to be a "good wife" and overlook the situation, but it's hard. Everyone knows that your husband wasn't exactly faithful. How did you put up with it?

Trying to Turn a Blind Eye

DEAR BLIND,

I didn't "put up" with the situation (as you so quaintly call it) if what that means is quietly enduring while pretending it wasn't happening. Rumor has it, I was very aware of my husband's infidelities and very angry. I figured out what I needed to tolerate his behavior. In my case it was money—heaps of money. I was set to divorce Jack until my father-in-law offered me a million dollars to stay in the marriage. I responded that if Jack gave me an STD, my price would be $20 million.[12]

If you're determined to stay in a relationship, you don't need to accept infidelity passively. Realize what could make it at least slightly more tolerable and name your price.

Keep your eyes open,

Jackie

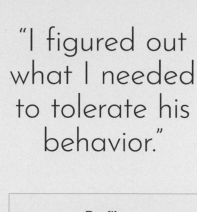

"I figured out what I needed to tolerate his behavior."

Profile
Married to JFK. The quintessential American First Lady. Looks great in a hat. (Given that nude photos of me, taken by the paparazzi, launched *Hustler* magazine in 1972, it's fair to say I also look great without a hat too.)

Turn-ons
Wealth, power, chic outfits

Turn-offs
Invasions of privacy, poverty, ugly outfits

HOW SHOULD YOU MEND YOUR BROKEN HEART?

1. Post breakup, what would you say your emotional state is right now?

A) So sad

B) So angry

C) Look, I'm just glad to be out of it.

D) Feeling pretty superior to him, honestly.

2. How would you describe your ex?

A) He did nothing to lessen my sense of being alone in the world.

B) OH MY GOD WHAT A DICK

C) I mean, he was fine, I guess? Though he's been a real ass since the breakup.

D) One of those guys who thinks he wants a strong woman, but absolutely does not.

3. What have you been eating lately?

A) Ice cream

B) Martinis

C) A normal diet, I guess?

D) Whatever I can get from the office vending machine.

4. And what are you listening to?

A) "Ain't "No Sunshine," Bill Withers

B) "We Are Never Getting Back Together," Taylor Swift

C) "Since U Been Gone," Kelly Clarkson

D) "I Am Woman, Hear Me Roar," Helen Reddy

5. Who is your ideal rebound?

A) I can't even think about it.

B) My ex's best friend

C) Someone tall, with a good sense of humor and kind eyes

D) Maybe someone who can cook my meals while I work late

6. Where is the best place to recuperate?

A) Someplace quiet, with the blinds drawn

B) One of those rage rooms where you can just break stuff with a baseball bat

C) Really, I keep telling you, I'm fine.

D) At work

7. Who else knows about your situation?

A) My closest friends and family members

B) My friends. My family members. My therapist. The postman. Everyone who read the blog post I wrote about the breakup.

C) Look, I hardly even told the man in question we were breaking up.

D) I mentioned it to a colleague in passing.

8. What's your go-to app?

A) Instagram, to stare at pictures of my ex and happier couples

B) Facebook, to share all my feelings

C) Tinder, for obvious reasons

D) LinkedIn

9. Do you think the breakup was in any way your fault?

A) I can be elusive and somewhat cold, perhaps.

B) MY ONLY FAULT WAS LOVING TOO MUCH

C) I don't think about it at all.

D) Hahaha, no

10. Do you think you'll ever love again?

A) I can't say.

B) IF I MEET SOMEONE WHO IS NOT A RAGING ASSHOLE

C) Yes. For the last and final time, I'm okay.

D) Maybe my job is my true love.

Mostly As:
Like Greta Garbo, maybe this is a time when you need to be alone. Breakups can be a time for quiet reflection. There's no need to rush back onto the dating scene. If you can, check yourself into a grand hotel of your own, where people will bring you breakfast in bed.

Mostly Bs:
Like George Sand, it seems that you don't have any positive emotions toward your ex. Maybe this is a good time to sit down at a typewriter and just vent all your feelings. Whether you turn it into a memoir is up to you.

Mostly Cs:
Like Oona O'Neill, you'll find leaving one bad relationship can free you up for a better one. Just remember to actually tell your ex that you are breaking up with them before you move on to that better one.

Mostly Ds:
Like Martha Gellhorn, your breakup has spurred on your working life. Maybe for you, the ultimate rebound is to be the best at your job in the entire world, and to inspire a younger generation of women. Stop looking for a romantic relationship, and start looking for your next mentee.

SINGLE LIFE

—

The after-dinner mints
that are to be savored
without sharing

Joan of Arc on

FILLING YOUR FREE TIME

DEAR JOAN,

One of the things I've noticed about single life is that the older you get, the more free time you seem to have, at least in comparison to the partnered-up people I see. When they're not working, my married friends are busy tending to their families. Meanwhile, I'm at a point in my career where I can have a more flexible schedule, and, when I come home, I can do whatever I want. Any thoughts on what I should do with that time? Travel? Volunteer? Work on a creative project?

Free as a Bird

DEAR BIRD,

Find a cause you are willing to *die for*. I would recommend leading an army for France in the name of Christ. Though this may sound like a hard thing to do, I pulled it off in my teens during the 1400s. It probably helped that Saints Michael, Margaret, and Catherine all spoke to me to help me find my way,[1] but, you know, maybe if you talk to God, he'll talk back.

The greatest problem in my mind is that even projects you love, like fighting your enemies, those heathens, may come to an end. During a truce between the British and French, I wrote a letter to those vile infidels, the Hussites, saying that I would relieve them of either their heresy or their lives.[2] Alas, I never got a chance to do so.

La Pucelle

"Find a cause you are willing to die for."

Profile
Religious crusader. Led the French army in the Hundred Years' War; burned at the stake when I was nineteen. Later canonized as a Roman Catholic saint. Some call me the Maid of Orléans. Others would say I'm just too hot to handle.

Turn-ons
The power of our risen Lord, fighting for France

Turn-offs
Infidels and open fires

101

Queen Elizabeth I on

HAVING DIFFICULT PARENTS

DEAR ELIZABETH,

I want to open my heart to love, but I just can't. I feel like I've put up a lot of barriers to happiness. In part, I think it might be because of the fact that my parents' marriage was horrible. Their eventual divorce really soured the whole idea of matrimony for me. I feel like I should have outgrown this. How can I get over my parents' bad relationship?

Wounded Daughter

DEAR WOUNDED,

Have you considered staying the way you are? Personally, I'd recommend focusing on keeping your heart, and therefore, your head. My mother, Anne Boleyn, had hers chopped off, by order of my father, King Henry VIII.

Even if there are fewer beheadings these days, love is still dangerous. It sounds like you figured that out early, as did I. By the age of eight, after seeing my father behead yet another wife, I declared that I would never get married. Nothing ever changed my opinion in this regard.

"I will have but one mistress here and no master,"[3] I told the Earl of Leicester, the man I probably came closest to loving, if not marrying. As for everyone else who wanted to marry me, I gave them "sweet words, but no promises."

Do you know how it worked out? Of course you do—I'm Queen Elizabeth. A movie will be made about me every ten years, for as long as there are people around to watch it.

Sincerely yours,
The Virgin Queen

"Focus on keeping your heart, and therefore, your head."

Profile

"I know I have the body but of a weak and feeble woman; but I have the heart and stomach of a king, and of a king of England too."[4] Looking for someone who has a similar heart and an appreciation of chalky makeup.

Turn-ons

Wigs, adventurers, strong hearts

Turn-offs

Weak and feeble men

Jane Austen on
SELF-SUFFICIENCY

DEAR JANE,

I feel that I am made for the single life. I enjoy sitting in my home with my cats, drinking tea, and reading classic novels. I have an income that allows me to lead my life the way I want. However, I know that I'm not having the kind of love affairs I've read about, and I wonder if I'm missing out on a large part of the human experience. You were single your whole life, but you wrote some of the most enduring romances of all time. Do you have any thoughts on whether a single life is preferable to a married one?

One Is Not the Loneliest Number

DEAR ONE,

Did you know that as a woman, you can inherit property now? Seriously, that's something that I'm just finding out and I'm very excited about it. If you read my books, you'll find that most of the women in them marry because they need to have a place to live. I don't really care about your cats or tea or reading material—although those all sound nice—so much as I care about the fact that you, a woman, can have an independent home and income of your own. With that taken care of, there's no need to marry unless you're super keen on the idea.

I told my niece in 1814 that anything is preferable to marrying without affection.[5] I took my own advice—I once had a marriage offer from a very eligible man, but changed my mind the morning after I accepted it. It sounds like in your situation there's less need to marry than ever, so do so only if you're wildly in love. Whatever happens, you can earn your own money—so who knows, you might finish up living on an estate that would be the envy of Mr. Darcy himself.

All my love,
Jane

"Anything is preferable to marrying without affection."

Profile
Nineteenth-century British author, a single woman of good fortune *not* in want of a husband. Not interested in any man who can't live up to Mr. Darcy. (For the record, I never found anyone who could.)

Turn-ons
Financial security, wit, wet shirts

Turn-offs
Scurrilous rogues and scoundrels

Mary Shelley on
GRIEVING

DEAR MARY,

My husband passed away a few years ago. I'm having a hard time letting go—at least that's what my friends and family tell me. It's been two years, and I still can't bring myself to get rid of any of his clothing, or some of his other personal items. I know I should, but I don't want to. Is it really so odd to keep a few items from your departed beloved?

Not Letting Go

DEAR NOT LETTING GO,

Ha ha ha, no, it's totally normal. Look, I was married to the poet Percy Bysshe Shelley and we ran away together when I was just 17 (we couldn't be properly married until later, after his first wife committed suicide). Tragically, he drowned six years later off of the Italian coast.

My dear husband was cremated. All of his remains burned—except for his heart. It was thought to have calcified and thus "resisted cremation as readily as a skull, a jaw or fragments of bone."[6] As e.e. cummings would write long after my own death, I carried his heart with me (though not in my heart—in a silk bag). After I died in 1852, his heart was found inside my desk, wrapped in the pages of his poem *Adonaïs*.[7]

So, that's how I handled grief. By comparison, keeping a few of your husband's old shirts seems downright quaint— pretty much the most normal thing you could possibly do, in fact.

Never let go,

Mary

"I carried his heart with me."

Emily Brontë on

WOMAN'S BEST FRIEND

DEAR EMILY,

I'm not interested in marriage or a family, but I am interested in getting a pet. I've moved into a building where they're allowed, and I can afford one. But I'm a bit worried that a dog or cat might be too much effort to care for. Also, if I start adopting animals, will I seem like too much of a "crazy cat lady"?

Trying to Avoid Getting Too Grey Gardens

DEAR GREY,

You should feel happy that I am writing to you at all. As one of my sisters said of me, "Though her feeling for the people round was benevolent, intercourse with them she never sought."[9] However, I will make an exception to tell you how pets are better than people.

My pets (including my hawk, Nero) have been a greater source of joy to me than any man or woman ever could provide. I once told my students that I much preferred the house dog to them (I only lasted as a teacher for six months...)[10]

And what if you do become a "crazy cat lady"? I would say that's a noble label, but then, I did take long walks where I conversed with animals and was quite sure that they understood me.[11]

You couldn't ask for a better companion to take long walks with, except maybe Heathcliff. And honestly, that's a strong "maybe."

With moderate affection,

Emily

"Pets are better than people."

Profile

Author of *Wuthering Heights*. Took libidos of young women to new heights. Personally, I have little interest in libido, though I would be up for long walks on the moors. Alone. Not with you.

Turn-ons

Painting, poetry, nature

Turn-offs

The company of others

Coco Chanel on

DEFYING EXPECTATION

DEAR COCO,

I'm single with a thriving career, but people will not stop judging me. Every time I go home for the holidays people start looking at me with huge, pitying eyes, and suggesting I marry a random man they know. My aunts and parents seem to have less interest in anything I'm doing professionally than they do in setting me up with someone. How do I convince them that I'm happy by myself?

On My Own

DEAR OWN,

There seems to be a general notion that a woman is not enough without a man. While it's understood that men might go out and do great things all on their own, it's assumed that a woman can do nothing greater than be someone's wife or mother. That's not true, and you should never let anyone pressure you into thinking it is. You can be great on your own.

If your family keeps pestering you, remind them that the Duke of Westminster once proposed to me, and a lot of people—including Winston Churchill—were excited by the prospect of that marriage, but I turned him down. It's often been claimed that I told him that while there had been several Duchesses of Westminster, there was only one Chanel![12]

And there was. I'm pretty sure you know more about me than you do about the Duke.

You're important enough on your own, and every woman should hold this as a truth in her heart. Over your heart—and your chest—you should wear a Chanel dress, obviously.

Adieu,
Coco

"You're important enough on your own."

Profile
Fashion designer. Creator of simple, modern, practical designs that made people focus on the woman, not the outfit. Looks good in a little black dress, and out of one.

Turn-ons
Men who want to look toward the future

Turn-offs
Men who want to confine women to the past

Simone de Beauvoir on
FREEDOM

DEAR SIMONE,

I can't help noticing that I see an endless variety of brilliant, accomplished women married to men who are not nearly their equals. It seems like someone being a "good wife" means that they're a great cook, doting mother, passionate lover, and able to maintain their appearance. Meanwhile, a "good husband" just seems to mean someone who does not cheat on his wife and has a job. Where's the fairness in that?

Better To Be Alone?

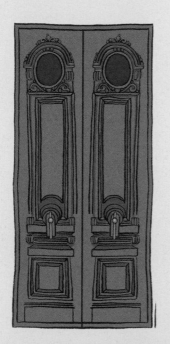

DEAR BETTER,

When I was 19, I wrote in my diary: *I don't want my life to obey any other will but my own.*[13]

Despite the fact that Sartre proposed, I turned him down, preferring, instead, to maintain an "essential" love with him that allowed for affairs on the side and separate housing. Marriage? Never. I think it's bad for men as well as women— forcing women to rely financially on men, and men to provide for women who detest them.

Until society changes—and we see a world where "Fathers should do just as much cleaning up. Just as there should be men nursery teachers, so that boys grow up thinking that a man looks after children, too"[14]— marriage will always be an unequal institution. Go out and, instead, form unions that work for you. Make sure they seem fair.

Go forth,
Simone

Profile
Intellectual. Equal. Anyone who thinks I was just Sartre's girlfriend is in for a surprise. *Second sex,* but unwilling to come second.

Turn-ons
Hot coffee, the classics, and conversation

Turn-offs
Confinement and conformity

"Marriage is bad for men as well as women."

Mae West on

REFUSING TO SETTLE

DEAR MAE,

I don't see much appeal in a long-term relationship. Sometimes this makes me feel like a freak, because it feels like everyone else does. But I like my life, and I like seeing a lot of men. But will I regret it when I'm older? My friends keep saying that if I play around too long, then eventually I'll end up alone. One of them even said that women have an "expiration date." Is it really the case that if I don't settle down, a time will come when no one is interested in me anymore?

Loving It

DEAR LOVING IT,

First off, your so-called friends sound like massive bores. I tried marriage, twice. Like I once said, "Marriage is a great institution. I'm not ready for an institution, yet."[15]

I promise you, age has nothing to do with being able to attract people. I was an on-screen sex symbol when I was into my 70s, and I never had trouble attracting younger men (like Cary Grant, for example, whose career I helped launch). I even starred in a movie called *Go West, Young Man*.

Paul Novak, with whom I had one of my lengthier affairs, was 30 years younger than me. And when The Beatles asked to use an image of me on their *Lonely Hearts Club* album cover, I replied, "What would I be doing in a lonely hearts club?"[16]

Frankly, I think the notion that you'll hit a certain age and stop being desirable is a conspiracy, concocted by dull men to make women marry them, when a girl might have much more fun being single with someone like ... well, any number of extremely muscled men. And remember—"Good women are no fun...The only good woman I can recall in history was Betsy Ross, and all she ever made was a flag."[17]

Love yourself and everyone else,
Mae

"Marriage is a great institution. I'm not ready for an institution, yet."

Profile

Bad girl who made good. I spent 70 years on-screen as a sex symbol and ten days in jail for "corrupting the morals of the youth." Hope you'll come up and see me sometime.

Turn-ons
Sex

Turn-offs
I'm always on

WHAT'S YOUR MUST-HAVE SINGLE-WOMAN ITEM?

1. How do you feel about going for long walks?

A) I honestly prefer driving, ideally in a convertible sports car.

B) I enjoy walking the city streets and taking in life around me.

C) I adore striding across the moors.

D) I'm more into reclining.

2. What are you reading right now?

A) A business book about how to get rich before you're forty

B) A feminist memoir

C) A book about the benefits of going vegan

D) Honey, I go to the movies.

3. What kind of music do you like?

A) Top 40 hits—anything that might wake me up in the morning

B) Classical music to inspire and focus me as I work

C) Indie bands like Fleet Foxes and Noah and the Whale

D) What genre is Barry White?

4. What's the trait you most dislike in yourself?

A) I can be a workaholic.

B) Sometimes I find it hard to get out of my own head and have fun.

C) I'm not very friendly.

D) I don't understand the question. Why would I dislike anything about myself?

5. And the trait you like best in yourself?

A) I'm self-assured and independent.

B) I'm a genius. That's just a fact, not a brag.

C) I'm a defender of the defenseless.

D) If I had to narrow it down to just one it would be my unrelenting sex drive.

6. Are you a morning person?

A) Yes. There's so much to do.

B) I'm a "late morning, sitting in a café" person.

C) I'm more into dusk.

D) Everything worth waking up for happens after midnight.

7. What kind of tree would you be?

A) A sturdy one with lots of branches

B) This is a nonsense question.

C) Any species—I would so love to be a tree!

D) One that offers comfort and fun to people underneath it.

8. What do you do at parties?

A) Network

B) Initiate deep, meaningful conversations

C) Talk to the dog

D) Flirt. Kiss in corners. Take over the host's bedroom, I'll use it better than they will.

9. What's your favorite game?

A) Monopoly

B) Trivial Pursuit

C) Scrabble

D) Twister

10. What's your favorite TV show?

A) Suits

B) Black Mirror

C) Can we just watch the Nature Channel?

D) Sex and the City re-runs forever

Mostly As:

You're going to need a gorgeous wallet. Get one of those really beautiful leather ones to hold all your credit cards, because, hey, you can make your own money and own property now. Jane Austen would be so incredibly impressed. No need to put up with some horrendous bore just to keep a roof over your head. Time to celebrate!

Mostly Bs:

You have such big ideas, you want to share them with everyone. You owe it to yourself to buy a top-of-the-line laptop. If Simone de Beauvoir were still alive, you know she'd bring her Apple Mac to the coffee shop to get down her next great manifesto. If the world can't have hers, it can at least have yours.

Mostly Cs:

You're going to need a huge purse. Not because you're hung up on material things, but because you're going to carry around a little dog in it, just like Emily Brontë would have done. You may also carry home other injured animals you find.

Mostly Ds:

Seems like you deserve a set of really expensive lingerie. Like Mae West, you're sexy and you know it. You deserve to show off your assets in the most beautiful set of underwear you can find. And you can celebrate your fabulousness for as long as the inclination takes you—either in front of the mirror, or in front of a young lover or two.

Endnotes

FLIRTING

1. Plutarch. *Caesar*, xlix. Loeb Classical Library. p. 559.
2. Clough, Arthur Hugh ed. *Plutarch's Lives: Of Themistocles, Pericles, Aristides, Alcibiades and Coriolanus, Demosthenes and Cicero, Caesar and Anthony*. New York: P.F. Collier. January 1, 1909. p. 340. http://bit.ly/2EpWZFK
3. Mendelsohn, Daniel. "Girl, Interrupted: Who Was Sappho?" *The New Yorker*. March 16, 2015. https://www.newyorker.com/magazine/2015/03/16/girl-interrupted
4. Tindle, Hannah. "Words More Naked Than Flesh": Ten of Sappho's Poignant Contemplations. *AnOther* magazine. March 7, 2018. http://www.anothermag.com/design-living/10653/words-more-naked-than-flesh-ten-of-sapphos-poignant-contemplations
5. Vale, Malcolm Graham Allan. *Charles the Seventh*. University of California Press. 1974. p. 94.
6. Angier, Natalie. "Goddesses, Harlots and Other Male Fantasies". *New York Times*. February 23, 1997. https://archive.nytimes.com/www.nytimes.com/books/97/02/23/reviews/970223.23angiert.html?_r=2
7. Vale. *Charles the Seventh*. p. 93.
8. Henley, John. "Scientific sleuth solves the riddle of what killed 'France's first bimbo.'" *The Guardian*. April 2, 2005. https://www.theguardian.com/world/2005/apr/02/france.jonhenley
9. Herman, Eleanor. *Sex with Kings: Five Hundred Years of Adultery, Power, Rivalry, and Revenge*, New York: William Morrow. 2004. p. 126.
10. Wilson, Harriette. *The Memoirs of Harriette Wilson, Volumes One and Two: Written by Herself*. London: Eveleigh Nash, Fawside House. 1909. Republished Project Gutenberg, 2013. http://www.gutenberg.org/files/43617/43617-h/43617-h.htm
11. Perrottet, Tony. *The Sinner's Grand Tour: A Journey Through the Historical Underbelly of Europe*. New York: Broadway Books. 2011. p. 85.
12. Arnold, Catharine. *Edward VII: The Prince of Wales and the Women He Loved*. New York: St. Martin's Press. 2017. p. 40.
13. Herrmann, Dorothy. *Helen Keller: A Life*. Chicago: University of Chicago Press. 1998. p. 193.
14. Eschner, Kat. "Three Big Ableist Myths About the Life of Helen Keller." SmartNews. Smithsonian.com. June 27, 2017. https://www.smithsonianmag.com/smart-news/three-big-ableist-myths-about-life-helen-keller-180963793/#wyUmIxfFTtQdkCmS.99
15. Herrmann. Helen Keller. p. 195.
16. Frías, María. "African-American Women Artists in Paris: Sex and Politics in Josephine Baker's *La Revue Negre* (1925) and Maya Angelou's *Porgy and Bess* (1954)," from *Nor Shall Diamond Die: American Studies in Honor of Javier Coy* edited by Carme Manuel and Paul Scott Derrick. Universitat de València, Departament de Filologia Anglesa i Alemanya. 2003. p. 143. http://bit.ly/2B3ZjOM
17. Ibid.
18. "Josephine Baker: The Life of an Artist and Activist." Al Jazeera. June 3, 2017. https://www.aljazeera.com/news/2017/06/josephine-baker-life-artist-activist-170602194956917.html
19. Blume, Mary. "Kiki of Montparnasse is Brought Back to Life." *The New York Times*. June 12, 1999. https://www.nytimes.com/1999/06/12/style/kiki-of-montparnasse-is-brought-back-to-life.html
20. Davis, Anna. "The Queen of Bohemia." *The Guardian*. February 7, 2007. https://www.theguardian.com/books/2007/feb/07/art.gender
21. Leigh, Wendy. *True Grace: The Life and Times of an American Princess*. St Martin's Griffin. 2007. pgs. 37 and 55.

GOING STEADY

1. Andrews, Evan. "Who Was Pope Joan?" History.com. June 10, 2015. https://www.history.com/news/ask-history/who-was-pope-joan
2. Schilling, Vincent. "The True Story of Pocahontas: Historical Myths Versus Sad Reality." Indian Country Today. September 8, 2017. https://indiancountrymedianetwork.com/history/genealogy/true-story-pocahontas-historical-myths-versus-sad-reality/
3. Townsend, Camilla. *Pocahontas and the Powhatan Dilemma: The American Portraits Series*. New York: Hill and Wang. 2004. p. 143.
4. Lucas, Emma. *Lucrezia Borgia*. New Word City. 2014. p. 149.
5. Griffin, Susan. *The Book of the Courtesans: A Catalogue of their Virtues*. New York: Broadway Books. 2001. p. 114.
6. Souhami, Diana. *Wild Girls: Paris, Sappho & Art: The Lives & Loves of Natalie Barney & Romaine Brooks*. New York: St. Martin's Press. 2004. p. 7.
7. "The 'Dollar Princess' and the Duke." Christie's Magazine, Old Masters Auction Preview. October 22, 2016. https://www.christies.com/features/The-story-of-Consuelo-Vanderbilts-marriage-to-the-Duke-of-Marlborough-7745-1.aspx
8. Serratore, Angela. "How American Rich Kids Bought Their Way Into the British Elite." Smithsonian.com. August 13, 2013. https://www.smithsonianmag.com/history/how-american-rich-kids-bought-their-way-into-the-british-elite-4252/#2PlmtTWSIaBes8mY.99
9. "Mrs. Balsan Dies." *The New York Times*. December 7, 1964. https://www.nytimes.com/1964/12/07/mrs-balsan-dies.html
10. Sebba, Anne. "We're Still Obsessed with Wallis Simpson". *The Telegraph*. January 20, 2012. https://www.telegraph.co.uk/culture/film/9025264/Were-still-obsessed-with-Wallis-Simpson.html
11. Dunlap, David W. "1932 | I'm Not 'Mrs. Putnam.' I'm Amelia Earhart." *The New York Times*. July 13, 2017.

https://www.nytimes.com/2017/07/13/insider/1932-im-not-mrs-putnam-im-amelia-earhart.html

12. "Amelia Earhart Biography". *Encyclopedia of World Biography*. Detroit: McGraw Hill. Gale Research, 1998. http://www.notablebiographies.com/Du-Fi/Earhart-Amelia.html

13. Diu, Nisha Lilia. "Zelda, Tragic Heroine Behind Scott's Classic". *Irish Independent*. February 8, 2009. https://www.independent.ie/lifestyle/zelda-tragic-heroine-behind-scotts-classic-26512067.html

14. Dickstein, Morris. "That irresistible couple". *The New York Times*. November 4, 1984. https://archive.nytimes.com/www.nytimes.com/books/00/12/24/specials/fitzgerald-mellow.html

15. Diu. "Zelda, Tragic Heroine."

16. Nin, Anaïs. Delta of Venus: Chapter 28. Gbnovels. http://www.gbnovelsonline.com/read/Delta-of-Venus-9025/99489

17. Glaister, Dan. "Lost Tape Reveals Marilyn's Inner Thoughts". *The Guardian*. August 6, 2005. https://www.theguardian.com/world/2005/aug/06/filmnews.film

18. "What Marilyn Said on the Secret Tapes". *Irish Independent*. August 7, 2005. https://www.independent.ie/woman/celeb-news/what-marilyn-said-on-the-secret-tapes-26211371.html

19. Meryman, Richard. "A Last Long Talk With A Lonely Girl". *Life magazine*. August 17, 1962. http://www.marilynmonroe.ca/camera/mags/life62.htm

MARRIAGE

1. Tacitus. Annals. Loeb Classical Library. 1937, p 295

2. Herman, Eleanor. *The Royal Art of Poison: Filthy Palaces, Fatal Cosmetics, Deadly Medicine, and Murder Most Foul*. New York: St. Martin's Press. 2018. p. 116.

3. Androutsos, George. "The Truth About Louis XVI's Marital Difficulties." *Progres en Urologie*, vol. 12. 2002. pgs. 132–137. History of Circumcision. http://www.historyofcircumcision.net/index.php?option=content&task=view&id=78

4. Covington, Richard. "Marie Antoinette". Smithsonian. com. November 2006. https://www.smithsonianmag.com/history/marie-antoinette-134629573/

5. Fraser, Antonia. *Marie Antoinette: The Journey*. New York: Anchor Books. 2002. p. 157.

6. Goodwin, Daisy. "Queen Victoria wouldn't be a poster girl for Mumsnet—but we could all learn from her refusal to feel 'mum guilt'." *The Telegraph*. August 23, 2017. https://www.telegraph.co.uk/women/family/queen-victoria-wouldnt-poster-girl-mumsnet-could-learn-refusal/

7. Ibid.

8. Staff. "7 People Suspected of Being Jack The Ripper." History.com. July 16, 2015. https://www.history.com/news/who-was-jack-the-ripper-6-tantalizing-theories

9. Goreau, Angeline. "Menage a Cinq." *The New York Times* Books. December 21, 1997. https://www.nytimes.com/1997/12/21/books/menage-a-cinq.html

10. Woloch, Nancy. "Eleanor Roosevelt's White House Press Conferences." National Women's History Museum. September 22, 2017. https://www.womenshistory.org/articles/eleanor-roosevelts-white-house-press-conferences

11. Storck, Kelly. *The Gender Identity Workbook for Kids: A Guide to Exploring Who You Are*. Oakland: New Harbinger Publications. 2018.

12. Leonard, Kevin. "Anderson, Lucy Hicks [Tobias Lawson] (1886–1954)." BlackPast.Org. http://www.blackpast.org/aaw/anderson-lucy-hicks-1886-1954.

13. Giovannini, Joseph. "DESIGN NOTEBOOK; In Painters' Poetic Homes, the Soul of a Nation Emerged". *The New York Times*. March 4, 1999. https://www.nytimes.com/1999/03/04/garden/design-notebook-in-painters-poetic-homes-the-soul-of-a-nation-emerged.html

14. Kahlo, Frida. "You Deserve a Lover." Words For the Year. November 13, 2017. https://wordsfortheyear.com/2017/11/13/you-deserve-a-lover-by-frida-kahlo/

15. Parsons, Russ. "Julie, Julia and Me: Now It Can Be Told". *Los Angeles Times*. August 12, 2009. http://www.latimes.com/food/la-fo-calcook12-2009aug12-story.html

16. Lowe, Lindsay. "Julia Child and Her Husband Made the Sweetest Valentine's Day Cards." Parade. May 1, 2018. https://parade.com/666423/lindsaylowe/julia-child-and-her-husband-made-the-sweetest-valentines-day-cards/

17. Chowhound Editors. "5 Things Julia Child Taught Us About Valentine's Day." Chowhound.com. January 25, 2016. https://www.chowhound.com/food-news/174996/julia-child-valentines-day-wisdom/

BREAKUPS

1. "Napoleon and Josephine: Crisis and Divorce". PBS.org. http://www.pbs.org/empires/napoleon/n_josephine/crisis/page_1.html

2. Douglass, Paul. *Lady Caroline Lamb: A Biography*. New York: Palgrave Macmillan. 2004. p. 120.

3. Castle, Terry. "Mad, Bad and Dangerous to Know." *The New York Times*. April 13, 1997. https://archive.nytimes.com/www.nytimes.com/books/97/04/13/reviews/970413.13castlet.html?_r=1&oref=slogin

4. Bair, Diedre. "Getting Even with Chopin." *The New York Times*. August 11, 1985. https://www.nytimes.com/1985/08/11/books/getting-even-with-chopin.html

5. MacPherson, Myra. *The Scarlet Sisters: Sex, Suffrage, and Scandal in the Gilded Age*. New York: Twelve. 2014. p. 181.

6. Renzetti, Elizabeth. "'Mrs. Satan': The first woman to run for U.S. president." *The Globe and Mail*. July 29, 2016. https://www.theglobeandmail.com/news/politics/mrs-satan-or-joan-of-arc-the-story-of-victoria-woodhull/article31199623/

7. Parker, Dorothy. Brendan Gill (Introduction). *The Collected Dorothy Parker*. London: Penguin Classics. 2001.

8. Ibid

9. Burk, Martha. "D-Day: 150,000 Men—and One

Woman." *HuffPost.* June 5, 2014. https://www.huffingtonpost.com/martha-burk/d-day-150000-men---and-on_b_5452941.html
10. Doucet, Lyse. "The Women Reporters Determined to Cover World War Two". BBC News. June 5, 2014. https://www.bbc.com/news/magazine-27677889
11. Hoffman, Barbara. "This New York Socialite Dumped J. D. Salinger for Charlie Chaplin". *New York Post.* September 7, 2017. https://nypost.com/2017/09/07/this-new-york-socialite-dumped-j-d-salinger-for-charlie-chaplin/
12. Porter, Darwin and Danforth Prince. *Jacqueline Kennedy Onassis: A Life Beyond Her Wildest Dreams.* Blood Moon. 2014. Kindle location 22000.

SINGLE LIFE

1. Castor, Helen. *Joan of Arc: A History.* New York: Harper. 2014. Kindle location 478.
2. Joan of Arc. Translated by Allen Williamson. "Joan of Arc's Letter to the Hussites." March 23, 1430. http://archive.joan-of-arc.org/joanofarc_letter_march_23_1430.html
3. Weir, Alison. "ELIZABETH I—THE VIRGIN QUEEN?" Random House.com. http://www.randomhouse.com/rhpg/rc/library/display.pperl?isbn=9780345425508&view=qa
4. "Elizabeth's Tilbury speech, July 1588." British Library. http://www.bl.uk/learning/timeline/item102878.html
5. Burstyn, Linda. "Words of Love." *The Washington Post.* February 13, 1996. https://www.washingtonpost.com/archive/lifestyle/1996/02/13/words-of-love/ab53d98b-0122-40d5-9692-8a11878eb3d1/?noredirect=on&utm_term=.f4dc6a8f2b0b
6. Selph, Alexa. "Shelley's Heart." *The New York Times.* August 6, 1995. https://www.nytimes.com/1995/08/06/books/l-shelley-s-heart-678095.html
7. Conradt, Stacy. "Mary Shelley's Favorite Keepsake: Her Dead Husband's Heart." Mental Floss.com. July 8, 2015. http://mentalfloss.com/article/65624/mary-shelleys-favorite-keepsake-her-dead-husbands-heart
8. Russell, Anna. "Early Feminists: Mary Shelley and Her Mom." *The Wall Street Journal.* April 22, 2015. https://www.wsj.com/articles/early-feminists-mary-shelley-and-her-mom-1429720017
9. *Life and Works of Charlotte Brontë and Her Sisters,* Charlotte Bronte, Anne Bronte and Emily Bronte. Wordsworth Edition. 2005. p. 720.
10. Hughes, Kathryn. "The strange cult of Emily Brontë and the 'hot mess' of Wuthering Heights." *The Guardian.* July 21, 2018. https://www.theguardian.com/books/2018/jul/21/emily-bronte-strange-cult-wuthering-heights-romantic-novel
11. "The Bronte Sisters." *Self Culture.* September, 1899 http://bit.ly/2Qmzx2B
12. Picardie, Justine. "Coco Chanel's Secret London World—and the Men Who Shared It." *Evening Standard.* September 16, 2010.

13. Moorehead, Caroline. "A talk with Simone de Beauvoir." *The New York Times.* June 2, 1974. https://www.nytimes.com/1974/06/02/archives/a-talk-with-simone-de-beauvoirr-marriage-is-an-alienating.html
14. Ibid.
15. Swainson, Bill. *Encarta Book of Quotations.* New York: Macmillan. 2000. p. 980.
16. Cashill, Robert. "Way Out West: Classic Lines from Hollywood's Dirty Blonde." Biography.com. August 15, 2017. https://www.biography.com/news/mae-west-quotes
17. Roberts, Steven V. "76—and Still Diamond Lil." *The New York Times.* November 2, 1969.

Author's acknowledgements

This book has not only been a love letter to women of the past, it's been one supported by so many amazing women of the present.

I'm so grateful to my friend Sarah Maslin Nir for connecting me with the lovely Camilla Morton, who chose to buy this book for Laurence King Publishing.

I've been blessed to work with Chelsea Edwards, who has been the most attentive and extraordinary editor through this whole process.

I owe so much thanks to my agent, Nicole Tourtelot for negotiating this deal and those for my other books.

This book also wouldn't be what it is without Carly Jean Andrews' gorgeous, vibrant illustrations and Mariana Sameiro's fantastic design.

Of course, thanks to my mom, Kathleen Wright, who will always be my first reader.

And, as a single exception from this female focused dedication, as always, endless thanks to my husband, Daniel Kibblesmith, best of husbands, best of men.